At Issue

Book Banning

Other Books in the At Issue Series:

At Issue

Book Banning

Thomas Riggs, Book Editor

GREENHAVEN PRESS
A part of Gale, Cengage Learning

GALE
CENGAGE Learning

Detroit • New York • San Francisco • New Haven, Conn • Waterville, Maine • London

Elizabeth Des Chenes, *Managing Editor*

© 2012 Greenhaven Press, a part of Gale, Cengage Learning.

Gale and Greenhaven Press are registered trademarks used herein under license.

For more information, contact:
Greenhaven Press
27500 Drake Rd.
Farmington Hills, MI 48331-3535
Or you can visit our Internet site at gale.cengage.com

For product information and technology assistance, contact us at

Gale Customer Support, 1-800-877-4253
For permission to use material from this text or product, submit all requests online at
www.cengage.com/permissions

Further permissions questions can be e-mailed to permissionrequest@cengage.com

Articles in Greenhaven Press anthologies are often edited for length to meet page requirements. In addition, original titles of these works are changed to clearly present the main thesis and to explicitly indicate the author's opinion. Every effort is made to ensure that Greenhaven Press accurately reflects the original intent of the authors. Every effort has been made to trace the owners of copyrighted material.

Cover © Images.com/Corbis.

LIBRARY OF CONGRESS CATALOGING-IN-PUBLICATION DATA

Book banning / Thomas Riggs, book editor.
    p. cm. -- (At issue)
    Includes bibliographical references and index.
    ISBN 978-0-7377-5554-1 (hardback) -- ISBN 978-0-7377-5555-8 (paperback)
    1. Censorship--Juvenile literature. 2. Censorship--United States--Juvenile literature. 3. Challenged books--Juvenile literature. 4. Prohibited books--Juvenile literature. I. Riggs, Thomas, 1963-
    Z657.B735 2011
    363.31--dc22
                                                                    2011014466

Printed in the United States of America
1 2 3 4 5 6 7 15 14 13 12 11

Contents

Introduction

Most Americans agree that the First Amendment right to freedom of expression is one of the most sacred provisions of the US Constitution, a cornerstone of American democratic values. Even so, Americans have wrestled over the limits of free speech throughout their history. Many books have been burned, banned, and suppressed on the grounds that they are obscene, seditious, or otherwise dangerous to the moral and political well-being of the public.

The first known instance of book burning in the United States dates to the colonial era. In 1650 William Pynchon, founder of the Springfield colony, caused an uproar when he published a religious tract that contradicted the established Puritan doctrine of the day. The book was confiscated, condemned in court as heresy, and burned in the Boston marketplace. Only four copies of the book survived, one of which is held today at the Connecticut Valley Historical Museum.

Banned for Obscenity

Legal grounds for censorship in America were first established in 1873 with the passage of the Federal Anti-Obscenity Act, or Comstock Law. Introduced by Anthony Comstock, founder of the New York Society for the Suppression of Vice (NYSSV), the law made it a crime to send "obscene," "lewd," "indecent," or "filthy" materials through the US mail. As special agent of the US Post Office from 1874–1915, Comstock presided over the confiscation of some 120 tons of printed material, including such works of literature as Aristophanes' *Lysistrata*, Geoffrey Chaucer's *Canterbury Tales*, and Giovanni Boccaccio's *Decameron*. In the decades that followed, the Comstock Law provided for the banning of works by Ernest Hemingway, Honoré de Balzac, Oscar Wilde, James Joyce, F. Scott Fitzgerald, Eugene O'Neill, John Steinbeck, and others.

Controversy surrounding James Joyce's *Ulysses* proved to be a watershed moment in the history of American censorship. The book was seized by US postal officials in 1920 and deemed obscene in a court trial the following year, making it illegal to publish in the United States. In 1933 the publisher Random House challenged the ban by attempting to import the novel into the country, and another trial ensued. This time federal judge John Woolsey decided that the novel did not violate obscenity law, as it was written with genuine artistry and would not lead a normal adult reader to depravity. Although the landmark ruling on *Ulysses* "broke the back of the Comstock Law," according to Claire Mullaly in a 2007 article in *First Amendment Center*, charges of obscenity would continue to threaten the US publication and distribution of many more books in the future, notably D.H. Lawrence's *Lady Chatterley's Lover*, Allen Ginsberg's *Howl and Other Poems*, and Henry Miller's *Tropic of Cancer*.

Banned as "Un-American"

In the United States, books have also been banned for political reasons. During the early 1950s anti-communist crusader Joseph McCarthy launched a campaign to purge "un-American" books from overseas libraries operated by the US Information Service (USIS). The removal and even burning of books overseas contributed to a wave of paranoia in the United States, where librarians and public school officials began to scrutinize textbooks and library collections for any materials that might be seen as "subversive."

In Indiana in 1953 the state Textbook Commission called for *Robin Hood* to be banned from public school libraries, charging that the story of a hero who robbed from the rich to give to the poor was insidious Communist propaganda. Although the Indiana state superintendent of education ultimately ruled against banning *Robin Hood*, elsewhere in the country, many other "dangerous" or "unpatriotic" books were removed from classrooms and libraries, including works by Steinbeck, Sinclair Lewis, Dalton Trumbo, and Mark Twain.

The Ongoing Saga of *Huckleberry Finn*

Mark Twain's *The Adventures of Huckleberry Finn* has been at the center of one of the most notorious and enduring censorship debates. During Twain's lifetime, the book was banned from libraries in Concord, Massachusetts, New Hampshire, and Brooklyn, New York, due to its coarse vernacular language—for example, using the word "sweat" rather than "perspiration." In recent decades, however, opposition to the novel has centered on Twain's frequent use of the word "nigger." Although scholars generally maintain that Twain's masterpiece is actually a satirical critique of racial prejudice in the antebellum South, parents in school districts around the country have pressed to have the book removed from libraries and reading lists on grounds that it is offensive and degrading to African Americans.

In 2011 the *Huckleberry Finn* censorship saga took an ironic twist when an Alabama-based publisher announced that it would publish a new edition of the novel in which hurtful racial epithets had been removed. While some applauded the move as a way to make the novel palatable to a wider audience, others were outraged, charging that "cleansing" the text merely constituted another form of censorship.

The Debate Continues

In the United States public school libraries enjoy significant First Amendment protections because of the *Pico* decision, a 1982 Supreme Court ruling that the First Amendment protects not only the freedom to express ideas but also the freedom to receive them. As such, according to *Pico*, it is unconstitutional to remove books from library circulation (thereby denying students access to these books) simply because certain parents or school officials do not agree with the ideas they contain.

In addition to the *Pico* decision, 1982 also marked the American Library Association's (ALA) first annual Banned Books Week, a national event that calls attention to the ongoing threat of book banning and affirms the importance of the Constitutional freedom to read. Significantly, it was in response to the repressive atmosphere of McCarthyism that in 1953 the ALA adopted its "Freedom to Read Statement," a declaration that the suppression of literature amounts to a denial of the basic premise of democracy—"that the ordinary individual, by exercising critical judgment, will select the good and reject the bad." Moreover, the statement reads, "Every silencing of a heresy, every enforcement of an orthodoxy, diminishes the toughness and resilience of our society and leaves it the less able to deal with controversy and difference."

Still, parents, religious groups, and other organizations "challenge" (or attempt to ban) hundreds of books every year, putting schools and libraries at the center of the country's so-called "culture wars." Those who bring challenges most often avow their desire to protect children from sexually explicit content, offensive language, and other "unsuitable" content. Those who defend these books insist that while parents have every right to decide what their own children may or may not read, no one has the right to determine what is suitable or appropriate for others.

In the first decade of the 21st century, the novels in J.K. Rowling's Harry Potter series were the most challenged books in the United States because of outcry from Christian groups over their treatment of witchcraft. In addition to focusing on such traditionally controversial young adult authors as Judy Blume, Robert Cormier, and Chris Crutcher, challengers also zeroed in on books that "normalized" homosexuality, most notably the children's picture book *And Tango Makes Three*, by Justin Richardson and Peter Parnell, in which a pair of male penguins hatch and raise a baby chick.

As the articles in this volume reveal, the subject of book banning is emotionally charged. In principle, the right to freedom of expression, as outlined in the First Amendment, seems like a democratic ideal that everyone could agree upon. But should it be absolute? In reality, there are many forms of written expression that could be potentially harmful, whether they promote hatred, offend a group of people, compromise national security, spread lies, or expose young readers to information they may not be mature enough to understand. When one considers the myriad individual scenarios in which a decision must be made about whether a certain book should be printed, distributed, purchased with public tax dollars, displayed on a shelf, or assigned in a classroom, it becomes easier to understand why people disagree. Recent disputes over literature about homosexuality vividly demonstrate how a book that is blasphemous to one person's religion might rescue another person from feelings of profound isolation and shame. While the debate over book banning continues to divide Americans, perhaps one thing everyone can agree upon is that books are powerful, often provocative, and may even change the way we think.

1

Censorship Cannot Be Allowed in America

Ellen Hopkins

Ellen Hopkins is the author of the bestselling Crank series for young adult readers as well as the poem "Manifesto," which was adopted as the official manifesto of the American Library Association's Banned Books Week in 2009.

Books dealing with edgy, dark subject matter such as addiction, abuse, suicide, and teen prostitution can offer young adult readers a broader perspective on the world, but these qualities often make such books and their authors a target for would-be censors. Self-appointed defenders of morality may attempt to force their views on the community by pressuring authorities to revoke a controversial author's invitation to a cultural event. Disinviting an author from an event because of disagreement over his or her ideas constitutes an act of censorship as defined by the National Coalition Against Censorship. Personal experience of such treatment led to the writing of "Manifesto," a poem adopted as the official manifesto of Banned Books Week in 2009.

On Tuesday [Sept. 28, 2010] I spoke to a packed house in Columbus, Georgia. I talked about my journey to *New York Times* bestselling author—a road pitted with pain. (My first novel, *Crank,* was inspired by my daughter's descent into the hell that is methamphetamine addiction.) Afterward, I signed books, and as the room emptied one lovely young woman remained. She came forward and when I asked her name, she crumbled into tears.

Ellen Hopkins, "Banned Books Week 2010: An Anti-Censorship Manifesto," *Huffington Post* (online), September 30, 2010. Copyright © 2010 by Huffington Post. Reproduced by permission of the author.

Then she shared her own story. How she started getting high in middle school, mostly as a way to deal with her alcoholic mother's absence. Didn't care about the trajectory she was on—straight down into the same hell my book represented so well. But one day, she found that book.

She saw herself in those pages, and suddenly knew she didn't want to be there. That book turned her around. Today she's been sober two years, is graduating high school and has embarked on a modeling career.

Readers Identify with Difficult Subject Matter

This wasn't a rare encounter. After almost every talk, one or more people wait until the room clears and tell me their story. And I have received tens of thousands of messages from readers, thanking me for turning them around, giving much needed insight, and even literally saving their lives. So I am more than a little saddened when my books are pulled from shelves, or even worse, when I am "dis-invited" from a speaking engagement.

Some call my books edgy; others say they're dark. They do explore tough subject matter—addiction, abuse, thoughts of suicide, teen prostitution. But they bring young adult readers a middle-aged author's broader perspective. They show outcomes to choices, offer understanding. And each is infused with hope. I don't sugarcoat, but neither is the content gratuitous. Something would-be censors could only know if they'd actually read the books rather than skimming for dirty words or sexual content.

Disinvitions Often Come from Those Who Have Not Read the Book

My first dis-invitation was last year in Norman, Oklahoma. I had donated a school visit to a charity auction. The winning bid came from a middle school librarian, who was excited to have me talk to her students about poetry, writing process, and reaching for their dreams. Except, two days before the visit, a parent challenged one of my books for "inappropriate content." She demanded it be pulled from all middle school libraries in the district. And also that no student should hear me speak.

The superintendent, who hadn't read my books, agreed, prohibiting me from speaking to any school in the district. The librarian scrambled and I spoke community-wide at the nearby Hillsdale Baptist Freewill College. (The challenged book, by the way, was later replaced in the middle school libraries.) The timing was exceptional, if unintentional. It was Banned Books Week 2009, and my publisher, Simon & Schuster, had recently created a broadside of a poem I'd written for the occasion. My "Manifesto" was currently being featured in bookstores and libraries across the country.

According to the National Coalition Against Censorship, removing an author from an event because someone disagrees with their ideas or content in their books meets the definition of censorship.

Segue to August 2010. Simon & Schuster repackaged "Manifesto" just about the time another dis-invitation took place. Humble, Texas is a suburb of Houston, and every other year the Humble Independent School District organizes a teen literature festival. I was invited to headline the January 2011 event. The term "invitation" would later be debated, as no formal contract was signed. But through a series of email exchanges, the invitation was extended, I agreed, we settled on an honorarium, and I blocked out the date on my calendar (thus turning down other invitations).

This time it was a middle school librarian who initiated the dis-invitation. Apparently concerned about my being in the vicinity of her students, she got a couple of parents riled and they approached two members of the school board. Again, no one read my books. Rather, according to the superintendent, he relied on his head librarian's research—a website that rates content. He ordered my "removal" from the festival roster, despite several librarians rallying in my defense.

Censorship Should Not Be Allowed in Any Form

According to the National Coalition Against Censorship, removing an author from an event because someone disagrees with their ideas or content in their books meets the definition of censorship. And in protest, five of the seven other festival authors—Pete Hautman, Melissa de la Cruz, Matt de la Pena, Tera Lynn Childs and Brian Meehl—withdrew. Our books are all very different. But our voices are united against allowing one person, or a handful of people, to speak for an entire community.

If you don't like content in a book, don't read it. If you don't want your child to read a book, take it away. But you do not have the right to decide "appropriateness" for everyone.

This year's TeenLitFest was canceled. None of us authors wanted that, or to punish the teens who wanted to see us. But this is a valuable lesson to the young people who are our future. Censorship cannot be allowed to flourish in America. If you don't like content in a book, don't read it. If you don't want your child to read a book, take it away. But you do not have the right to decide "appropriateness" for everyone. What's perhaps not right for one child is necessary to another. Ignorance is no armor. And those whose lives are touched by the issues I write about deserve to know they are not alone.

And so, in honor of Banned Books Week 2010, I give you:

Manifesto

To you zealots and bigots and false

patriots who live in fear of dis-
course.

You screamers and banners and
burners

who would force books

off shelves in your brand name

of greater good.

You say you're afraid for children,

innocents ripe for corruption

by perversion or sorcery on the
page.

But sticks and stones do break

bones, and ignorance is no armor.

You do not speak for me,

and will not deny my kids magic

in favor of miracles.

You say you're afraid for America,

the red, white, and blue corroded

by terrorists, socialists, the sexually

confused. But we are a vast quilt

of patchwork cultures and multi-
gendered

identities. You cannot speak for
those

whose ancestors braved

different seas.

You say you're afraid for God,

the living word eroded by Mu-
hammed

and Darwin and Magdalene.

But the omnipotent sculptor of
heaven

and earth designed intelligence.

Surely you dare not speak

for the father, who opens

his arms to all.

A word to the unwise.

Torch every book.

Char every page.

Burn every word to ash.

Ideas are incombustible.

And therein lies your real fear.

2

Parental Concerns About Book Content Should Not Be Dismissed

Suzanne M. Beasterfield

Suzanne M. Beasterfield is an English instructor at Dixie State College of Utah. Her areas of interest include parent-teacher interactions regarding literature and curriculum.

Most people have strong opinions on the subject of parental involvement in deciding what books their children should study in school. While teachers vigorously defend the right to intellectual freedom, parents are just as passionate in pleading their right to help decide what their children may read. A teacher should therefore be sensitive to the parents' values and expectations as they relate to choosing appropriate reading material for students. Although some might argue that exposure to strong language, violence, or sexuality is simply a part of real life, these elements may be far removed from the real lives of students who are raised in the strong religious traditions of the Mormon church (the Church of Jesus Christ of Latter-Day Saints). It might be tempting to deride a parent's attempt to shield his or her child from negative portrayals of life and reality, but the parent's desire to present the child with positive portrayals is not so easily dismissed. Similarly, although students should not restrict their reading to material that portrays their own race, class, or religion, they should be able to find at least something familiar in the material they read.

In the ancient city of Nara, Japan, there is a huge building called Todaiji that houses a giant Buddha. The Daibutsu, as he is called, sits serenely surrounded by swirls of incense in the semi-lit room. He's enormous—big enough that a grown person could crawl into his nose. At the beginning of every methods class I teach, I show students pictures of the Daibutsu and his house, and I ask my future English teachers the crucial question, "Which is bigger, the Buddha or the building?" The mostly white, middle-class American students typically tell me that, logically, the building is bigger because the Buddha fits inside. I point out to them what many Japanese might tell them: The Buddha is sitting down. If he stood up, he'd be much bigger than the building. The lesson to be learned is that both answers are right; it is simply a matter of perspective. I have tried to instill in students a tolerance for different ideas, values, and identities, and I have generally regarded myself as a pretty tolerant person, but I have decided I wasn't seeing the whole picture when it came to parent-teacher clashes over literature in the classroom.

My philosophy became (and still is) that just as everyone has the right to read, view, and hear what they want, everyone has the right not to read, view, or hear what they don't want.

In the last few years I have been studying what happens when parents don't agree with what English teachers ask their children to read. Most of the time this doesn't involve censoring a book completely (i.e., removing it entirely from the school or library). Most of the protesting parents are concerned primarily with what their own children are reading. In reading, teaching, and researching this issue, I have yet to come across anyone who doesn't have a strong opinion on the topic. My friends in academia and my fellow teachers have strenuously asserted their support of literature and the right to read, and the parents I interview have just as passionately pleaded for their right to help decide what their children need.

I do draw a line and do believe some things are not fit for youth—but my line is in a different place than many of the parents of the teens I taught.

As a high school teacher in a predominantly LDS [Church of Jesus Christ of Latter Day Saints, commonly called the Mormon Church] community, I knew better than to assign *The Catcher in the Rye* [by J.D. Salinger] to students; the parents would never consent to it. I did not, however, anticipate that I would have parent protests over virtually every book I tried with my tenth graders. My philosophy became (and still is) that just as everyone has the right to read, view, and hear what they want, everyone has the right *not* to read, view, or hear what they don't want. I also had to concede that parents have a right to decide what their children will or will not read. That meant that if I couldn't convince a parent that a book was worth reading, I would offer a suitable alternative— even if I did not agree with the parent's decision. It became my habit to give students who rejected a book an independent unit on *Fahrenheit 451* [by Ray Bradbury], my subversive way of saying something on the subject of burning books. No one ever seemed to catch my little joke. Most of my colleagues agreed that pulling a student from class while others worked on a certain book wasn't an ideal solution, and we all worried that parents would take things further and attempt to censor the books—keep them out of our classrooms and off our library shelves altogether.

Negotiating Mormon Values

Even though I grew up LDS in a fairly conservative community, I have not adopted the sometimes-severe attitudes of many conservative parents. I believe that everyone draws lines—Who would consider *Playboy* appropriate for a first-grade classroom library?—but we draw them in different places. I believe everyone censors things, but I consider some forms of censorship dangerous. For example, I chafe at the idea of keeping our fully qualified teachers from ultimately making decisions about which books should be read in their classrooms. I also don't think one parent ought to decide that what doesn't work for his or her child won't work for the rest of the class or school. I fully respect parents' right to be involved in their own children's education—in fact, I applaud and encourage involvement—but I have lamented when parents have chosen not to let their teens read books that I personally deem important. I am not a parent and I cannot say how parenting would change me, but I hate to see kids whose parents put a gag order on all reasonable adults in their lives so that they have no choice but to get their "dirt" from other sources. I do draw a line and do believe some things are not fit for youth—but my line is in a different place than many of the parents of the teens I taught.

As a teen I was one of those "good kids" who never smoked, never did drugs, didn't drink alcohol. I was in a public school that granted one period per school day for "released time" to attend religion classes we called seminary. I went to seminary every day without pressure from my family. But I was a curious kid, too. When a teacher mentioned *The Catcher in the Rye* and said that she couldn't let us read it, I did what I'm sure she wanted me to and got myself a copy. I loved the book. I remember that it articulated something in me that I felt but couldn't express. Now I wonder how the book would have affected me if one of my English teachers had been able to guide me through it.

As an adult I see why parents wouldn't want their children to read it. Mormons don't believe in sex outside of marriage, and a book in which an adolescent hires a prostitute would definitely fall under the category of "not part of Mormon values." I have heard many teachers disparage parents' attempts at preventing their children from reading; they say that they are saying worse in the halls, seeing worse on television and in the movies. While this may be true in some cases, it is also true that most LDS parents do not tolerate swearing nor do they allow their children to see R-rated movies, and many parents restrict their kids from PG-13 movies and some television. I was sometimes able to gain ground and make a case for books in my classroom by reducing the novel to mass media terms: "Mrs. Smith, I assure you that *Of Mice and Men* [by John Steinbeck] doesn't contain anything beyond a PG rating or certainly anything near what is shown on network television." But what could I do for those students who aren't allowed to watch even network television?

Trying to Persuade Conservative Parents

I have heard—and been part of—the arguments on the other side. Students will access this stuff even if their parents disapprove, they *need* exposure to "real" life, and so on. The only problem is that some of these topics—such as adolescent sexual experimentation and substance use or abuse—simply are *not* real life to every teen, and their parents will tell you they don't need to hear about them. I have made the argument that the dark side of humanity is real and ought to be explored, that good guys don't always come out on top, that one can be "in the world but not of the world" as the scripture goes, but that one ought to know the world in order to navigate it successfully. These are some of the things I wanted parents to see.

My initial plan was to come up with a nifty guide to show parents why they ought to consider allowing their children to read great books that might not be G rated. I armed myself with the "Students' Right to Read" document from NCTE [National Council of Teachers of English] and with Joni Richards Bodart's lovely explanation of how to write a rationale for teaching a book. I told myself that reasonable adults might be swayed if my arguments were persuasive enough. That changed just a bit one Sunday, when a woman at church approached me with a problem. She told me that her daughter was supposed to be reading *The Catcher in the Rye* starting the next day, and that she had asked for an alternative but that the new book—something I had never heard of—was "too graphic" to be acceptable. Could I, this parent wondered, help her find a suitable alternative to suggest to the department chair the next day? I jumped at the chance—here was a field test of my idea before I even finished the guide.

I went home and racked my brain for titles. I came up with a short list and called the woman later that evening. We had an interesting discussion. I had gratefully dived into this task believing that *The Catcher in the Rye* is not essential to a teenager's education and that there were other well-written coming-of-age books that would do. Unfortunately this woman didn't stop at Salinger: she wanted to know if there were alternatives to *Lord of the Flies* [by William Golding] (a personal favorite of mine), *Of Mice and Men* ("Couldn't my children avoid Steinbeck altogether?" she asked), and *A Prayer for Owen Meany* [by John Irving]. I tried my best defenses for each of the books. I felt that my argument for *Lord of the Flies* was particularly persuasive, but she didn't budge.

The biggest irritation I felt, however, was the nagging idea that this essentially closed-minded person still did have a point . . . .

I turned the conversation around. What was she looking for? Not all of the books she was resisting were sexually explicit, particularly violent, or full of profanity. She answered that she felt that so much of high school literature took people to a dark place. Even if one puts a positive spin on the themes, they are still heavy and dark. She wanted happy endings, inspirational stories that left one feeling good at the end. She wanted books that showed people experiencing punishment and remorse for bad behavior (her primary issue with *Lord of the Flies* was that even the bad boys were rescued). She wanted her children to continue to love reading—as they had when they were younger—and she felt that the school's curriculum was damaging their love of books.

Rethinking the Teacher's Position

I have to say that part of me understood her position. I remember thinking, even as a young English major, that literature is only canonized if it is depressing. I was still shocked and even a bit offended at the extent of her rejection of high school literature, but this was an articulate, educated person. She had read the books in question and still didn't want her child to read them. This damaged one of my theories—that if parents just read the books they would see some of the value and see how little the "offensive" parts matter. The biggest irritation I felt, however, was the nagging idea that this essentially closed-minded person still did have a point, darn it all. Just as there is evil in this world, there is good. Just as there are tragedies, there are happy endings. Just as there is darkness, there is light. Where is the light in our classrooms?

I don't believe every book is worth reading or has equal merit in the classroom, and I don't believe we should be reading books simply because they have been banned.

The question in my mind changed from "How do I justify these works?" to "Why do we choose what we do in English classrooms?" I'm not saying that any of the works we teach in schools are not worthy—their language, characterization, themes, and so on are worthy, indeed—but how could I answer a parent who asked if there wasn't something just as brilliantly written that showed her values? The canon has already been attacked for years on the basis of its exclusion of works written by women, for example, or for failing to represent the experiences of other marginalized peoples. And here was a mother telling me that her experience and her story were not being told—that she was one of the people in the margins. We are becoming aware (and rightly so) of issues regarding race, sexual orientation, and class, but are we still shying away from some margins? This makes my little parent guide a bit more complicated. I don't think that students should read books that portray their particular religion, class, or race exclusively; that kind of relativism seems as dangerous as fitting everyone into the same mold. After all, one of the best reasons to read is to understand other people and places. But if a mother can't see *anything* of herself or her worldview in the books her son or daughter is reading at school, that's a problem, too.

Avoiding Polarization

I am currently a teacher educator in an English department, and a few years ago a group of student teachers did a class presentation about censorship. The first presenter, a cheerful, articulate, smart young man in his mid-twenties, began his remarks by saying that any parent who wouldn't allow his or her child to read any book was a "wacko." I was horrified as the students belittled or dismissed the opinions of their students' parents without consideration for what the parents were saying or why. Suddenly my attitudes as a teacher were being mirrored back to me in an ugly way. The students talked about Banned Book Week and enthusiastically advocated for banned books based solely on the notion that we ought to read them *because* they have been censored. I felt that I had failed these students. Somehow, instead of making them champions for literature, I had turned them into bullies for books. So much for my soapboxes on culturally responsive teaching! I don't believe every book is worth reading or has equal merit in the classroom, and I don't believe we should be reading books simply because they have been banned. How had this crucial point been missed by my students?

Then I thought that perhaps our English teachers need help articulating the reasons for their choices of novels, but now I'm not sure that is the answer. Would a speech from a teacher justifying the merits of his or her curriculum help Hispanic American parents feel better about their children's reading only works by and about dead, white males? Then why do I feel it would help in the case of conservative, religious parents?

I wish I could just convince the mother who spoke to me at church and others like her that these books are worthwhile. I chafe at censorship, and I think any LDS parent should, too. We are a religion, after all, whose founder was tarred and feathered while his printing press was destroyed and he was ultimately martyred for his religion. We should know all about the dangers of censorship. Just a few summers ago an undoubtedly well-meaning congregation in Michigan barbequed a pile of Harry Potter books and copies of the Book of Mormon—one of our religion's works of scripture. I am concerned when *any* voice is silenced—whether written or spoken. This issue goes beyond whether or not a girl who saw [the movie] *Titanic* four times ought to object to Robert Cormier's discussing how a girl's breasts look in *I Am the Cheese*. This has to do with whether we as English teachers have thought about why we are teaching what we are. Do we choose books because they are what we were taught? Do we just choose what's available, what the school bought? This may be our reality. But we have a responsibility, nonetheless, to thoroughly interrogate our curriculum and to make sure we know *why* we are arguing that a few *damns* and *hells* are worth reading to get to the heart of Steinbeck, and why little English boys murdering each other on an island is worth discussion. We can also never stop asking whose voices *aren't* being heard in our classrooms, and what we can do to change that.

I tell future teachers now that they need to do a lot more listening before they dismiss a parent's concerns.

Encouraging Open-Mindedness on Both Sides

I'm still going to work on my parents' guide. I once had a teacher who said that restricting access to things only teaches teens that they are weak and can't handle the world. He wanted his children to grow up with the message that they are strong and able to judge for themselves. I want to get this message out. I still think there is something to be said, starting with helping students to read critically and with discernment. Then again, this kind of critical literacy is just as important for teachers—maybe even more so.

This doesn't mean that I will quit advocating for worthwhile works that are pulled from the shelves so that no one can read them. It doesn't mean I will tell student teachers to cave to every whim of every parent, or to concede their expertise in choosing works that matter. It means that I refuse to simplify the issue of what students ought to be reading and who ought to decide. I'm not going to use the war vocabulary that I hear too often when parents and teachers talk about dealing with each other—we teachers talk of "arming" ourselves to "battle" with parents, for example. It means that I will try harder to hear all the voices of those who have a stake in educating students, and I will try harder to help students have opinions without denying others their right to have them as well. I tell future teachers now that they need to do a lot more listening before they dismiss a parent's concerns. What are parents really asking for when they say no to a book? How can we accommodate reasonable requests without compromising our curriculum? My student teachers role-play being parents and teachers in conferences, and I think this helps them to better understand the parents' perspectives as well as practice how to communicate tactfully with them. I ask my student teachers to spend more time thinking about and articulating the merits of the literature they teach so that they can make better-informed decisions about what to teach and how to defend their choices. I think that the Buddha in his building would be pleased—whether he's sitting or standing.

3

Book Challenges Bring Attention—and More Readers—to Many Great Books

Pat Scales

Pat Scales is a retired school librarian, author of Teaching Banned Books: 12 Guides for Young Readers, *and a national spokesperson on intellectual freedom for young people.*

A number of books for young readers have run afoul of would-be censors, and as a result, works such as In the Night Kitchen *by Maurice Sendak have virtually disappeared. But many others, including Sendak's* Where the Wild Things Are, *have become best sellers, often because of the censors' attempts to eliminate them. Whereas the references to menstruation in Judy Blume's* Are You There God? It's Me, Margaret *are now considered acceptable, the theme of masturbation ensures that* Deenie, *another book by Blume, remains a target of challenges. Gay and lesbian, occult, and anti-religious themes have made* Heather Has Two Mommies, *the Harry Potter books, and* The Golden Compass, *respectively, focal points of opposition by conservative groups. Yet as these and other examples show, banning a book can also help spur its sales.*

Max imagined himself into the land of the wild things, and the censors said *no*. Mickey fell out of his clothes in full-frontal view, and the censors said *no*. When [author] Judy

Blume gave Margaret her period, gave Tony Miglione wet dreams, and answered Deenie's questions about masturbation, the censors said "too much information," and they said *no*. When [author] William Steig turned donkey Sylvester into a rock and sent his parents to the pig policemen for help, the censors called these, respectively, an "out-of-body experience" and "offensive to law enforcement officers," and they said *no*. And when [author] J.K. Rowling sent Harry Potter to the Hogwarts School of Witchcraft and Wizardry, the censors called it "evil," and they said *no*.

Some Subjects Will Always Be Controversial in Children's Literature

Max is almost fifty years old, and the censors have finally put him to bed and left him to dream his way to *Where the Wild Things Are* [by Maurice Sendak]. Now approaching forty, Mickey hasn't been so lucky. Many children have never seen [Sendak's] *In the Night Kitchen* because adults are just too troubled by nudity. There are a few grownup children who remember reading the book but say they never noticed that Mickey was naked. It's likely that the boy they knew wore pajamas, or perhaps a diaper, designed by teachers and librarians using opaque magic markers. Never mind that the text reads that Mickey "fell through the dark, out of his clothes / past the moon & his mama & papa sleeping tight."

Most censors have now recovered from the idea that fictional characters can have periods . . . But there are still those who consider the topics of wet dreams and masturbation taboo.

Those who were uncomfortable with Maurice Sendak's *In the Night Kitchen* are now causing a fuss over Dav Pilkey's Captain Underpants series. "There's just not a place in children's books for underwear," remark those who challenge the books. Some assert that boxer shorts would be more appropriate than the jockey shorts the Captain proudly wears. Children are amused by underwear, which is one of the reasons that Pilkey's series is so popular. And it's all different styles of underwear that attracts young readers to *The Philharmonic Gets Dressed* by Karla Kuskin. Though this book has eluded censors in recent years, it did raise eyebrows when it was first published in 1982. Censors saw no reason for underwear to "ruin" a book about musical instruments.

Most censors have now recovered from the idea that fictional characters can have periods and Judy Blume's *Are You There God? It's Me, Margaret* is as popular with young girls today as it was when it was published in 1970. But there are still those who consider the topics of wet dreams and masturbation taboo. For this reason, [Blume's novels] *Then Again, Maybe I Won't* and *Deenie* continue to be challenged, especially in schools where computerized reading programs are used. These programs determine the readability level of books with no regard to maturity level. Parents then complain when their "gifted" second and third graders come home with books that are targeted for older readers. The Alice series by Phyllis Reynolds Naylor; *It's Perfectly Normal: Changing Bodies, Growing Up, Sex, and Sexual Health* by Robie H. Harris and Michael Emberley; *Where Willy Went . . .* by Nicholas Allan; and many other books about sexuality appear on the American Library Association's most challenged books list.

Censors Often Target the Latest Social Issues

Novels and picture books featuring gays and lesbians are now the biggest targets of censors. *Annie on My Mind* by Nancy Garden had its day in court in Kansas in the 1990s; more recently, *Daddy's Roommate* by Michael Willhoite and *Heather Has Two Mommies* by Lesléa Newman have been the topic of heated discussions on talk radio shows across the nation. *And*

Tango Makes Three by Justin Richardson and Peter Parnell is the latest book to cause debate on this subject.

Fantasy is another matter, though Steig's *Sylvester and the Magic Pebble* no longer causes a stir. Not since the 1970s has anyone cared that the policemen in the book are portrayed as pigs. And only a few adults understand (or remember!) the concept of an "out-of-body experience"; to young readers, Sylvester's magic pebble is simply a magic pebble.

The Harry Potter books remain troublesome to some adults, especially the Christian right. They object to any book that challenges their "Christian views" and believe that children who are exposed to witches and wizards may be tempted to engage in "evil" activities themselves. *The Golden Compass* and other titles in Philip Pullman's His Dark Materials trilogy have had similar problems. Critics have called the books antireligious and demanded that they be removed from public and school libraries. When the Catholic League called upon the public to boycott the film version of *The Golden Compass*, challenges to Pullman's entire series escalated.

Social issues are red flags for censors.

Sometimes Censors Blame Books for Society's Ills

Violence in children's books is another topic that gives censors pause. *Killing Mr. Griffin* by Lois Duncan, a favorite novel of middle school readers, had been on library shelves for years when the Columbine tragedy occurred. Struggling to make sense out of that massacre, the censors began blaming books, and novels such as *Shattering Glass* by Gail Giles and *Give a Boy a Gun* by Todd Strasser quickly fell under the watchful eyes of parents and nervous school administrators. Now, Neil Gaiman's *The Graveyard Book*, winner of the 2009 Newbery Medal, is already being labeled by some as too violent and ghoulish for young readers.

Profanity, racial epithets, and any type of name-calling in children's books almost always bring protest. *On My Honor* by Marion Dane Bauer, *Blubber* by Judy Blume, *Anastasia Krupnik* by Lois Lowry, *Fallen Angels* Walter Dean Myers, *Shiloh* by Phyllis Reynolds Naylor, and *The Land* by Mildred D. Taylor have fallen prey to censors for one or all of these reasons.

It is human nature to want to read what others say you shouldn't, and banning a book often helps keep it in print for years.

Social issues are red flags for censors. They don't like books that deal with bullying, child abuse, drug and alcohol use, death, gangs, rape, war, or any topic that causes young readers to contemplate the world's ills. Ironically, censors who wish to control what children read question the controlled society in *The Giver* by Lois Lowry. Jonas is a hero, but censors don't care. They see only the issue of euthanasia, and they say *no*.

Almost any book can fall under the guillotine of censors. The good news is that challenges bring attention to some great books. It is human nature to want to read what others say you shouldn't, and banning a book often helps keep it in print for years. The (tongue-in-cheek) moral of this story for writers: call upon young readers' imaginations by creating stories filled with magic, witches and wizardry, nudity, profanity, sex, violence, and social issues. And don't forget the underwear. The censors may say *no*. Young readers will say *yes*.

4

Teens Need Bold Books

Don Gallo

Don Gallo was an English professor at Central Connecticut State University for more than twenty years and has edited numerous anthologies of short stories for young adults.

The tendency of some individuals and groups to place controls on what others may learn is cause for alarm. Those who advocate such controls do not trust teenagers to make the right decisions. They often call for the banning of books without actually reading them, and even in rare instances where objecting parents have read the books in question, they fail to see beyond the sometimes controversial language and to appreciate the valuable message in many such works. Individual preferences are understandable, and parents have a right to restrict what their own children read, but they should not control the choices available to other people's children. Most such challenges come from members of the Christian Right, who selectively read and interpret the Bible. In order to respond to such challenges effectively, teachers of literature must be bold thinkers who are not afraid to offend.

I prefer to think independently rather than follow any group's party line. That applies to education, religion, politics, and a number of other organized things. I own the unfortunate curse of wanting to know the reasons for things—the *whys* and the *hows*. And I want sensible answers. Which is

Don Gallo, "Censorship, Clear Thinking, and Bold Books for Teens," *English Journal*, vol. 97, no. 3, January 2008. Copyright © 2008 by National Council of Teachers of English. Reproduced by permission.

why the kind of group-think that seems to be behind so many book challenges bothers me. Given a choice between group-think and independent thinking, I expect sensible people to choose independent thinking. But in America (not to mention Iraq, Iran, and other countries) a scary proportion of individuals prefer to be told what to think, what to believe, how to act. And what to read.

Book Banners Are Distrustful and Controlling

Whether it comes from fear of different ideas or from a need for power over others, most challenges to books used in schools and provided in libraries come from individuals and groups that do not want young people to make decisions for themselves. Comments I have heard and read from book banners suggest that they do not want their children to open their minds to new and different possibilities, do not want them to consider other points of view, do not want them to *think*. They do not trust teenagers to make right choices. And they do not trust educated teachers and librarians who have dedicated their lives to helping kids find the books they need for their intellectual development and emotional well-being.

Several years ago, a parent in a Connecticut school district objected to five literary works that were required reading in eighth grade: Robert Cormier's *The Chocolate War*, Bette Greene's *Summer of My German Soldier*, Robert Newton Peck's *A Day No Pigs Would Die*, Paul Zindel's *The Pigman*, and Robert Cormier's short story "In the Heat" from my first anthology, *Sixteen*—all considered today to be young adult classics. When asked if she was "aware of the judgment of this material by critics," the mother's response to each book was a variation of "I don't care what awards it won—I don't place value in what the critics say." That is only one parent's response, of course. But the published records of objections to books provide many more examples. Worse, many would-be censors act as if English teachers and librarians are immoral manipulators intent on subverting the values that are being taught at home. And as other records show, many of those parents and other "concerned" citizens make their decisions about the books in question without reading them.

That parent in Connecticut also declared that *she* is the best judge of what is acceptable for her children to read. She may be right about that. Right or wrong, she does have the legal obligation to protect her children and so has the right to restrict what they read. But, like most other objectors to books and other media, the concern of this mother did not stop with her children. She wanted those literary works removed from the curriculum so that *no* eighth grader would be required to read them.

[M]any would-be censors act as if English teachers and librarians are immoral manipulators intent on subverting the values being taught at home.

That's pretty much the way book censorship works, except in this instance the school and district's administration did not remove those books just because one parent objected. They followed the guidelines for reconsidering instructional materials; they valued the judgments of their English and reading teachers, who had selected those titles for good reasons; they assembled a folder of reviews and awards the books had received; and they had a series of public hearings where students as well as adults could express their opinions. In the end they chose to reaffirm the value of those books in their eighth-grade program.

Concerned Parents Often Miss the Point

Although this event occurred seventeen years ago, I chose to recount it not just because it had (from my perspective) a happy outcome or because the school district did all the right things in dealing with the objections. I chose it also because the case had one unusual element: the objecting parent had actually read each of the books, including additional stories from *Sixteen*. As a result, the mother was able to identify the parts of each work that she and her husband found objectionable, noting the page of each reference, except for *The Chocolate War*, where the mother admitted to reading only the first 139 pages of the 253-page book because she "couldn't stomach anymore." Fair enough. She obviously read those 139 pages carefully, because she was able to note every instance of the words *bastard, hell, bullshit, breast,* and *goddamn* along with other comments and concepts she and her husband found objectionable. They did the same for each of the other texts.

Though they read the *words* carefully, their written comments indicate they missed the intentions of the words, the themes, the concepts. They did not see—or *feel*—those more significant things. They saw only what they wanted to see. In Cormier's short story, for example, they ignored the tenderness between father and son and the comfort that love can bring during the painful process of dealing with the death of the wife/mother. Instead, they saw the pain of death, the strong words, and what they viewed as inappropriate role models for children. They saw disrespect for a teacher and the absence of good role models in *The Pigman*; offensive language and the father's verbal abuse of his daughter in *Summer of My German Soldier*; the gore and the sad deaths in *A Day No Pigs Would Die*. Those negatives for them outweighed any positive attributes the books had.

OK—certain things turn off certain people. My wife refuses to read any book in which an animal dies. Some readers won't read a book where characters curse. Lots of readers won't touch science fiction, others fantasy, especially if the novel has a witch or wizard in it. Many readers want only books with happy endings. Lots of people want only books in which the good guys and gals win every time. Most of us hate books where the lead character isn't likeable. These are emotional and not intellectual responses. No one has control of anyone's emotional response to a story. And in the final analysis, our emotional response is the only thing that matters when we read, no matter how much some literary critics might want to dispute that.

Though they read the words *carefully . . . they missed the intentions of the words, the themes, the concepts. They did not see—or* feel—*those more significant things.*

Books Containing Mature Content Must Be Read in Context

Many critics of contemporary young adult books, like the parent in Connecticut, attack them because they often contain violence, evil, and various examples of bad behaviors. Others attack books like these because they see the books as opposed to their religious beliefs. In fact, the majority of attacks on books in the last few years have come from what has been called the Christian Right.

People who take the Ten Commandments literally, for example, are repelled every time a character in a book says *ohmygod*. People who believe in the reality of witches freak out over the fictional wizardry in the Harry Potter books. Many of those people hold up the Bible as the best (or only) example of literature they want children to read, ignoring the fact that the Bible overflows with sex, violence, treachery, betrayal, theft, adultery, incest, bigamy, illegitimacy, and mayhem. People in the Bible, in fact, are killed in as many creative ways as one can find in any of today's supermarket tabloids: stabbed, slashed, stoned, hanged, burned to death, nailed to crosses, and in one instance a spike is driven through a man's temple, pinning him to the floor. Isn't that lovely?

In the last two years, a number of well-known Christian clergy as well as laypeople have led vicious attacks on books for teenagers that contain gay characters because the biblical book of Leviticus says that being gay is an "abomination." It also says that such offenders should be killed. I do not dispute that claim—the Bible does say that (twice) in Chapters 18 and 20 of Leviticus. Why, then, do I criticize this? Elsewhere in Leviticus it also orders, among other things, that adulterers should be put to death; believers should not eat pork—or rabbit, camel, tortoise, shellfish, and snails, among other creatures; men are forbidden from having their hair trimmed; and wearing clothing made from more than a single kind of thread is forbidden. Other books of the Bible approve of concubines and slaves, and a passage in Exodus says that anyone who works on the Sabbath shall be put to death. I need not go on. Why do so many people, then, ignore all those other admonishments yet choose to attack gay people and books with gay characters on the basis of what the Bible says?

I don't believe you can be an effective teacher of literature without being a bold thinker.

The Bible is an amazing collection of fascinating stories (except for the begats part), but they must be viewed intelligently and the sordid parts must be viewed in their context. So must the events in *A Day No Pigs Would Die*, and [William Shakespeare's] *Macbeth*, and the Harry Potter books, and every newly published book for teens that has been reviewed in this column.

Teachers and Librarians Must Consider the Needs of All Students

That is why anyone who edits a column like this one must be bold in his or her thinking. And it's why language arts teachers and librarians must be open-minded souls who think independently and consider the possible needs of *all* students, including those from religiously conservative homes. I don't believe you can be an effective teacher of literature without being a bold thinker.

Not too long ago I received an email from a high school English teacher in a small town in Wyoming who was disturbed by the books I had recommended in my July 2006 column. (Among the titles were Chris Lynch's National Book Award Finalist *Inexcusable*, Mary E. Pearson's touching *A Room on Lorelei Street*, Ellen Wittlinger's insightful *Sandpiper*, Markus Zusak's clever *I Am the Messenger*, and Jan Cheripko's beautiful *Sun Moon Stars Rain*.) I don't know whether the correspondent read any of those books, but the descriptions I provided led him to believe that it is books like those that cause our society to have "problem[s] with teen pregnancy, under age drinking, drugs, etc. . . . With this kind of filth running around in their brains, its [*sic*] no wonder we produce the kind of kids today. Please recommend some good books that teach good values and morals for today's youth."

To be able to face life outside their protective homes and classrooms, teenagers need access to books that allow them to see the bigger world.

I see no difference between the parent in Connecticut who wanted various books removed from the eighth-grade classroom and this Wyoming teacher who didn't want his high school students to even know about the kinds of books I had recommended. Both people are concerned about their teenagers; both want to protect the kids. But neither of the adults seems to respect their teenagers, and neither seems to believe that teens, unlike the adults, have the good sense to see the positive attributes of any of those books.

I wrote back to that teacher, pointing out that teen pregnancy, underage drinking, and other ills of society have existed for far longer than books like those I reviewed in my July column. There is obviously no cause and effect there. On the contrary, I said, "I believe those books provide excellent moral values for teenagers, even those from Wyoming. If nothing else, *Inexcusable* is about moral responsibility. *Sun Moon Stars Rain* is one of the most beautiful moral stories I've read in a long time. *Sandpiper* provides teens with several moral lessons, as does *I Am the Messenger.*" I wondered if the teacher objected to those books because there was an element of sex in each of them. If that's why any teacher keeps books out of the hands of high school teenagers, they don't understand teenagers and aren't willing to help them deal with one of the most important aspects of their lives.

Good Books Are Those That Challenge Us to Think

Similarly, I have heard and read comments from too many school librarians who, fearing to upset a parent or an administrator or the majority of adults in their community, are afraid to order certain books. In an effort to not offend one individual or even many, they ignore the needs of others. I've heard too many librarians ask for "safe" books, books that won't cause a controversy. I'm proud to say that I don't think this column under my editorship has ever recommended a book that is without controversial elements. The column is titled "Bold Books" for a reason. Good books have always caused people to think, and since few of us think alike, controversy is guaranteed. To be able to face life outside their protective homes and classrooms, teenagers need access to books that allow them to see the bigger world. And there's no better place to explore the larger, diverse, often scary world than from the safe distance a book provides. Denying teenagers access to a controversial book denies them a better future.

Teens need books like those reviewed in this column, not only for their intellectual, emotional, and moral growth but also for the hope that if today's kids can become comfortable thinking for themselves, the future of this country will be better served. So we must be bold and courageous in our choices of books and in our teaching. And maybe in the future there will be fewer attacks on books because today's teens will be tomorrow's adults who better understand the value of diverse viewpoints and experiences.

5

Parents Must Protect Children from Offensive Material in Books

Erin Manning

Erin Manning is a Fort Worth, Texas-based writer who maintains a blog called And Sometimes Tea.

If true censorship were an actual threat in the United States, all reasonable people would support the goals of Banned Book Week. The real aim of the American Library Association (ALA), however, is to subvert the authority of parents and place control over children's education in the hands of the school system. Gone are the days when parents could trust schools and libraries to uphold their values; today quite the opposite is true, and in fact the ALA goes out of its way to support even substandard books as long as they promote its social agenda. Modern educational life is characterized by a cultural divide between families on the one hand and powerful organizations such as the ALA on the other. Parents are therefore justified in teaching their children not to give educators and librarians their unqualified trust.

During the last week of September every year, the American Library Association [ALA] holds what it calls "Banned Book Week." The purpose of this week, the ALA says, is to highlight ". . . the benefits of free and open access to information while drawing attention to the harms of censorship by spotlighting actual or attempted bannings of books across the United States."

Erin Manning, "It's Not Censorship, It's Parenting!" *MercatorNet* (online), November 17, 2009. Copyright © 2009 by MercatorNet. Reproduced by permission of the author.

It sounds like a noble endeavour, right? In this day and age I think it would be hard to find people who would actively support the notion of outright censorship. Yet we know that at other times and in different kinds of regimes around the world this dedication to free speech has not always been the rule. Keeping the principle of free speech safe requires vigilance; if people in America really were seeking to ban books—to forbid their printing or sale, for instance—it would be important to focus on their efforts and to raise awareness about them.

But that kind of "banning" isn't what the ALA is talking about at all.

The ALA Misrepresents Parental Concerns

In fact, according to their website, the ALA's Banned Book Week is really called "Banned and Challenged Book Week." A "challenge" to a book occurs when someone objects to some of the content of a book, and, most of the time, asks that the book be removed from children's access. Parents were responsible for 57% of such challenges between 1990 and 2008, and an astonishing 70% of the challenges involved books that were either in a school classroom or a school library. Moreover, nearly a third of challenges made to all books (including books aimed at adults) were made because the challengers found the materials to be too sexually explicit.

Now, if the vast majority of challenges to books involve parents, centre around books available in schools, and deal with such issues as sexual explicitness, offensive language, or the unsuitability of the books for a specific age group, then I think we're no longer talking about book-banning or censorship. I think we're talking about parenting.

The attitude of the ALA is that a parent only has the right to censor or control what his own children read. He doesn't have the right to request the removal from the school library or classroom shelf those books which he finds obscene or dangerous to morality, because someone else might prefer for his children to read those books. The school alone has the final say in what books are appropriate for the children under its care to read, and if a child reads at school a book or books which his parents absolutely forbid at home—well, then, perhaps the parents' values are too narrow and restrictive to begin with.

[M]ost of these books are not, frankly, works of much merit at all.

Some Books Are Challenged for Good Reason

Here's the dilemma for parents, though—there was a time when we could trust schools and libraries to support, for the most part, the same values we ourselves held, and to abide by community standards of morality and decency. There was a time when it would have been just as unthinkable to the librarian or the school teacher as to a parent that a book for children would have contained the following things:

- Graphic language about sex, drinking, drugs; laced with profanity and written in "chat speak" (*TTYL* by Lauren Myracle)

- Violence, implied sex, anti-religious and anti-Christian messages throughout; God is literally killed (His Dark Materials, Philip Pullman)

- Prostitution, witchcraft, voodoo, devil worship (*Bless Me, Ultima* by Rudolfo Anaya)

- Homosexuality, drugs, suicide, sex, nudity (*The Perks of Being a Wallflower*, by Stephen Chbosky)

- Sex, drugs, alcohol, eating disorders, profanity, smoking (Gossip Girl series by Cecily von Ziegesar)

These are some of the objectionable content found in just five of the ten most frequently challenged books for 2008. Given that most challengers are parents and most challenges involve books in school libraries or school classrooms, I'd be much more worried about society if books like these were never questioned at all.

Many of the challenges to these books are due to their presence on middle school bookshelves (or even in class assignments); middle school students can be as young as eleven years old. And yet the ALA views parental challenges to these books as being somehow akin to book-burnings and government censorship, as if there were no legitimate reason why a group of parents might not want their children reading novels in which gratuitous and explicit sex, violence, drug use, and the like were major elements of the story.

It is clear that in many instances the library and the school, as political entities, no longer share the cultural values of the vast majority of parents.

Contemporary Young Adult Literature is Often Mindless and Sensationalized

The fact is, there are plenty of good reasons to object to books with these content elements in them, especially when such young children are the ones who have access to these books. Even if the works rose to great literary heights parents would not be out of line to ask that they be moved from the middle school library; but most of these books are not, frankly, works of much merit at all. They are the fiction equivalent of mindless TV programs, complete with pandering, fantasy, commercialised writing, and shock value in place of decent storytelling, a well-developed plot, interesting and three-dimensional characters, and some idea of consequences for actions.

To put it bluntly, the ALA puts itself in the position of defending lousy, substandard, second-rate writing that would probably not even be published in the first place, were it not for the insatiable appetite for inappropriate content usually euphemised as "dark" or "edgy" by the sort of pre-teen who thinks angsty, brooding, sparkly vampires are a good idea. And they cast parents in the role of villains, as if their well-founded concerns about the content and merit of these books were on a par with Nazi book-burning efforts.

Parents Can No Longer Count on Libraries and Schools to Share Their Values

It is clear that in many instances the library and the school, as political entities, no longer share the cultural values of the vast majority of parents. We are living through a time of cultural divide—and whether you think it's a good or a terrible idea for novels aimed at eleven-year-olds to contain sex and violence—is largely going to depend which side of that divide you and your family is on.

Because we no longer live in a world where it would be unthinkable for an authority figure to give a child a book in which depictions of sex, violence, drug use, profanity and the like are major elements, it is no longer safe to delegate the choice of reading material for our children to such entities as the school teacher or school librarian. Because we no longer live in a time where giving a child a book like that would be considered either child sexual abuse or contributing to the delinquency of a minor, but instead is supported with smiling approval by the moral midgets at the ALA, parents have to be more vigilant than ever. Because we no longer live in an era where we can trust the authority figures in our children's lives to share our values and foster the same view of morality and decency which we ourselves have, we can't afford to let our children read whatever trashy novel they pick up at school.

It isn't censorship, to teach our children that they can't trust their teachers or librarians to give them good, wholesome books. It's just the fallout from our fractured culture, which insists on calling evil, good—and then handing it to children.

6

Homophobia Is at the Root of Many Book Banning Efforts

Mel Seesholtz

Mel Seesholtz is a professor of English at Pennsylvania State University, Abington.

The American Family Association and other conservative Christian organizations have a history of mistreating homosexuals and spreading homophobia. Such groups often cite the US Constitution and the Bible when advancing their claims against gay people and in favor of parents' rights to deny their children exposure to homosexuality. The Constitution makes no mention of such rights, however, and the Bible offers an explicitly pro-homosexual agenda. Adults from these purportedly Christian organizations teach youths the un-Christian lesson that homosexuals deserve to be tormented. In order to sustain this aversion to homosexuals, anti-gay activists often destroy books with homosexual content. History has shown that such acts are common among people who fear knowledge and truth.

L ike all "irrational fear of, aversion to, or discrimination," homophobia is a learned behavior. It feeds on hate and the desire to do harm to fellow citizens that have been reduced to abstractions or objects of disgust.

Don Wildmon's American Family Association [AFA] is well-known for its anti-gay boycotts. They try to hurt American businesses that treat their gay and lesbian employees equally. They turn people into targeted objects of disdain and fodder for their malevolent "cause." . . .

The legal arm of the AFA is the Center for Law and Policy. Steve Crampton is its chief counsel.

"Unless the people of the State of Massachusetts rise up with one voice in opposition to this lawless and socially destructive behavior, it will destroy society as we know it," said Crampton, following the Massachusetts Supreme Court decision acknowledging civil marriage equality.

When the University of Florida began offering health care coverage to same-sex domestic partners—all 25 couples who initially signed up—he had this nonsensical response: "Steve Crampton, chief counsel with the American Family Association Center for Law & Policy, says, in this case, homosexuality appears to be the preferred lifestyle of the State of Florida."

In his latest missive—"Poison In Our Libraries"—Crampton and the AFA Center for Law and Policy again taught the lesson of irrational fear of, aversion to, and discrimination toward the gay and lesbian Americans.

Laurie Taylor is the mother of two school age children in Fayetteville, Arkansas. She discovered some books in the school library she objected to. Naturally, they had to do with the reality of homosexuality and that homosexuals are people "just like you and me."

She demanded the school place the books in a "parent library" section. She and like-minded others formed "Parents Protecting the Minds of Children." Not exactly a descriptive name. "Parents Closing the Minds of Children" or "Parents Perverting the Minds of Children" would have been more accurate.

"Constitutional Right" to Sequester Books Does Not Exist

Not surprisingly they found other books they objected to and demanded the school not make them available to students without parental approval. Many of the books they targeted had won awards, including "outstanding book for children." The school refused their request to censor.

Crampton and the AFA Center for Law and Policy were quick to join the fight for irrational fear of, aversion to, and discrimination: "The AFA Center for Law & Policy has agreed to represent Taylor and other Fayetteville parents in a federal lawsuit seeking *to protect their constitutional rights* to oversee the education of their children." [italics added]

Crampton's own words: "All Taylor and the other parents asked for was that the books be placed in a restricted access section, thereby allowing parents to exercise their *God-given (and constitutionally protected) rights* to oversee the moral upbringing of their children." [italics added]

By arguing books that reference homosexuality or contain "gay" characters should be sequestered, the lesson being taught is that "gays" are bad people to be mocked, shunned, or otherwise tormented.

Unlike Crampton, I do not presume to speak for God or know Her will, but I can read. The United States Constitution does not contain the words "parent" or "parents," "moral" or "morality."

The Christian Reich and their legal eagles adamantly advocate the philosophy of "originalism" and "textual literalism" when it comes to interpreting the Constitution, especially in relation to the separation of church and state, free speech, the civil equality of all Americans, and the right to privacy. So from whence does this "constitutional right" of which Crampton speaks come?

Restricting "Gay" Books Sends a Bad Message

What Crampton's Center for Law and Policy are really doing is teaching homophobia. By arguing books that reference homosexuality or that contain "gay" characters should be sequestered, the lesson being taught is that "gays" are bad people to be mocked, shunned, or otherwise tormented. British educationalist Mark Jennett recently made the case at a conference in London, as reported by the BBC:

> Mr Jennett said figures showed 81 percent of primary school pupils identified the use of the word "gay" as "a means of attacking or making fun of someone."
>
> He added: "By the time they find out that it means to be homosexual, they have already learnt that it means something bad." . . .
>
> He said: "We should talk about sexuality, not sex: things like people's family lives.
>
> "Primary school children are very strong on the concept of fairness. We should tell them just how unfair homophobia is."

The same lesson was taught by the Alliance Defense Fund (ADF), a kindred organization to the Center for Law and Policy. The ADF was founded by a group of ultra conservative Christians, including Dr. James Dobson and Dr. D. James Kennedy, both infamous for their homophobic crusades. Threatening a lawsuit the school could ill afford, ADF forced Springfield High School in Oregon to allow a student to wear a T-shirt emblazoned with the message "I am a Christian, and I am against homosexuality, abortion, pre-marital sex, and drugs." What's the *definitively* non-Christian message being taught about gay and lesbian students?

In the gospels Jesus said *absolutely nothing* about homosexuality, abortion or drugs. But he did—with Mary Magdalene at his side—call upon the faithful to dedicate themselves to creating a more ethical and just world and to assuring justice and equality for all "God's children," especially the disenfranchised. Bishop Gene Robinson was blunt and true to the gospels when he told reporters he believes "gay rights" are consistent with Christian values and that "Jesus is the agenda, the homosexual agenda" of equality for all God's children.

Homophobia Is Un-Christian

But the ultra-conservative Christian Reich is obsessive-compulsive . . . about teaching irrational fear of, aversion to, and discrimination toward gay and lesbian Americans:

> "Hundreds Protest Allowing Textbooks to Include Gay Information"
>
> Written for the web by Elizabeth Bishop, Internet News Producer
>
> Hundreds of members of conservative and religious groups rallied [in 2006] at the [California] State Capitol to urge legislators and the governor to reject bills they say will indoctrinate public school children. They are especially upset about a bill that would require lessons on positive contributions of gays and lesbians in history.

Apparently reality and history offend the self-righteous who wish to exclude, shun and demonize some of the most prominent men and women in American and world history. What are the lessons these protesters and their actions are teaching American youth?

It's the same message the Christian Reich proudly proclaimed when $300,000 for construction, expansion and renovation of the Gay and Lesbian Center in Los Angeles was axed by "pro-family" Republican representative Steve King of Iowa. His amendment to the funding bill says "none of the funds made available in this act [a Transportation, Treasury, Housing and Urban Development appropriations bill] shall be for the construction, renovation or building of the Los Angeles Gay and Lesbian Center."

If his amendment doesn't pass, King says others in the House may vote down the entire bill because of the provision.

What's the message Rep. King is teaching the country's youth? The answer is simple: gay and lesbian Americans *and their families* don't count. Shun them, demean them, exclude them.

Anti-gay activists trade on lies about gay people and our families. Books and information are the first things they want to target.

Book Burning Reveals Fear of Knowledge

What America's youth are learning is that the agenda of the "Christian Right" is anything but Christian and that the "pro-family" label is anything but pro-family. And those are lessons worth learning, especially in the historical light cast by burning books:

"Fire started in library's gay books section"

June 15, 2006

By Annie Sweeney, Crime Reporter

Chicago Police are investigating a suspicious fire that burned about 100 books from the gay and lesbian selection at a North Side Chicago Public Library branch.

The fire—definitely deemed arson—was set days before a gay pride parade and walk in Chicago, the city hosting Gay Games VII that, despite feverish efforts and boycotts by the Christian Reich, continue to gain major corporate sponsors, the latest of which are ESPN and QTG, the maker of Quaker Oats, Tropicana juice and Gatorade.

The morning after the blaze, Rick Garcia, public policy director of Equality Illinois, said that he had little doubt about the motivation: "Anti-gay activists trade on lies about gay people and our families. Books and information are the first things they want to target."

Germany, 1930s: book-burning was also a favorite pastime of those who feared knowledge and truth. How far we *haven't* come . . .

7

Librarians Must Be Prepared to Defend Their Selection Criteria

Connie O'Sullivan and Michael O'Sullivan

Connie O'Sullivan is an information specialist at Eastview High School in Apple Valley, Minnesota. Michael O'Sullivan is an instructional media coordinator at Rosemount High School in Minnesota.

Librarians should be on guard against attempts at manipulation by gifts of books that promote views other than those recognized by science. A particularly significant battleground in recent years is the topic of intelligent design, a latter-day form of creationism that cites the complexity of the universe as evidence of a creator. By rejecting books deemed unworthy, librarians may find themselves in lengthy battles with opponents who portray them as censors rather than guardians of intellectual freedom. Librarians should therefore educate themselves on the distinctions between censorship and selection, and between popular and scientific literature. With anti-evolution legislation under consideration by numerous state legislatures, it is imperative that librarians be prepared for such challenges. They need to understand the creationism controversy, know their opposition, contact the National Center for Science Education (NCSE), and plan their strategies. Librarians should also update their district's gift and selection policy, explain their policies before accepting gifts, respond to all charges of censorship, organize wide-ranging support, and confront assaults on quality instruction and library resources.

High School librarian Cora Kunkle never ordered *Of Pandas and People* for her collection, but 60 copies ended up in her library's collection anyway. The textbook, promoting intelligent design as an alternative to evolutionary theory, was given anonymous to Pennsylvania's Dover Area School District last year, and placed in the Dover Senior High School media center on the order of Superintendent Richard Nilsen.

Media specialists often defend controversial books. But what if the tables were turned and we were branded as censors for rejecting unworthy books?

It turns out that William Buckingham, the chair of the school board's curriculum committee, had solicited donations at his church to help pay for the books and one of the donors happened to be the father of the school board president, Alan Bonsell. This eventually led to the board voting in favor of introducing intelligent design into the ninth-grade biology curriculum—the issue that lies at the heart of *Kitzmiller v. Dover Area School District*, the landmark lawsuit involving 11 Dover parents who are suing their school district for teaching what they say is religious creationism under the guise of scientific theory. The trial is the most significant court challenge to evolution since 1987, when the Supreme Court prohibited the teaching of creationism in public schools, ruling that it was not science but religion and violated the separation of church and state.

While the outcome of the Dover case, which is likely to be settled this month[1], will influence the way science is defined

1. On December 20, 2005, the court ruled that it is unconstitutional to teach intelligent design in Dover public schools.

and taught in our nations classrooms, librarians are just as concerned with another matter: how to handle the increasing number of donated books on intelligent design theory that have little or no value to our students and come from those with ulterior motives.

Media specialists often defend controversial books. But what if the tables were turned and we were branded as censors for rejecting unworthy books? That's exactly what happened to us five years ago.

Back in 2000, as high school librarians in Minnesota's suburban Independent School District 196, we received donated copies of *Darwin's Black Box* by Michael Behe and *Darwin on Trial* by Philip Johnson, both of which champion intelligent design. Although advocates of design theory—the concept that the universe is so complex that it must have been created by an unidentified intelligent being—don't specifically mention God, they suggest that various forms of life began abruptly, with their distinctive features already intact; fish with fins and scales, birds with feathers and wings, and mammals with fur and mammary glands.

Donated Books Must Meet Standard Selection Criteria

We want to make one thing clear: both of us are firm supporters of the First Amendment and of students' rights to access information—but only if that information is credible. Intelligent design lacks scientific validity and has been repudiated by every leading scientific organization, including the American Association for the Advancement of Sciences and the National Academy of Sciences, both of which asset that design theory lacks any scientific merit and cannot be supported by scientific research. Teaching it would be tantamount to teaching about the existence of Santa Claus.

At the time, we didn't realize that the motive behind the parent's book donations was to include intelligent design in the science curriculum. Free books or not, our district's gift policy states that all donations intended for instructional use must meet certain selection criteria—they must support the curriculum, receive favorable reviews from professional journals, and be age-appropriate.

Both books struck out on all counts. We found them difficult to comprehend without having an advanced background in biology, and neither was reviewed by a standard review source for high school materials, such as *Kliatt* magazine. They also received mediocre reviews from *Library Journal* and *Publishers Weekly. Choice,* a book review source for academic librarians, said the books were appropriate for advanced academic or graduate school biology students. Even reviews from scientific journals such as *Nature, Scientific American,* and the *Annual Review of Anthropology* said the books refuted well-established scientific discoveries involving evolution and were flawed in their scientific analyses, hypotheses, research, and conclusions. Consequently, we rejected the books.

Explaining the difference between popular and scientific literature, as well as the difference between selection and censorship were key elements in our presentations to the board of education.

Donors May Challenge the Library's Decision

That wasn't the end of it. The donor brought the matter before the school board, accusing us of censorship and insisting that the decision be reversed. Unexpectedly, the board changed its policy and established a reconsideration process to appeal gift rejections—effectively overruling our decision to refuse the two books. Suddenly, we were caught in a lengthy battle that made us look like censors.

The issue went to a reconsideration committee, made up of teachers, parents, and students. The committee heard arguments from the donor stating we were censoring materials and that we should be required to place both books in the high school libraries. We stated the books did not meet the district's selection criteria and did not support the curriculum.

In spite of these arguments, the committee apparently accepted the censorship argument and voted to reverse the high school librarians' decision and allowed *Darwin on Trial* in the library. Just prior to the vote on the second book, *Darwin's Black Box*, a member of the committee abstained, resulting in a tie vote, which upheld our decision to reject the gift offer. Both decisions were appealed to the board of education.

Explaining the difference between popular and scientific literature, as well as the difference between selection and censorship were key elements in our presentations to the board of education. An area scientist explained to the board the difference between popular and scientific literature, stating that since intelligent design is not a scientific theory, the results of an online search only turned up references to products being "intelligently designed." In fact, a current search of scientific literature today only brings up articles that point out the fallacies of the intelligent design theory.

Like it or not, librarians are going to be caught in the middle of this battle between science and religion, and we must prepare to defend our collections from the influence of pro-creationist groups.

Deciding Not to Select a Book Is Different from Censorship

In a prepared statement to the board, Patricia Sween, president of the Minnesota Coalition for Intellectual Freedom, wrote, "The process of selection means that some items are not selected when they do not meet the criteria as well as other sources do. Decisions to not select items cannot be equated to censorship." We also argued that students still could obtain information on intelligent design from newspapers, magazines, and professional journals accessible through the library's databases and book catalog. Local scientists, an ophthalmologist, concerned parents, high school science teachers, and two ministers all spoke to the board on our behalf.

After three long months, our fight to preserve quality science paid off. The board understood that we were not censoring materials, but simply choosing to select credible materials, and they voted to support our decision to keep both books out of the high school libraries.

As religious conservatives continue to gain a stronger voice in our political climate, librarians must be on guard: supporters of this 21st-century version of creationism are making advances. Just this year alone, 18 states have either introduced or are considering anti-evolution bills in their legislature, according to the National Center for Science Education (NCSE), an organization that defends the teaching of evolution in public schools. Like it or not, librarians are going to be caught in the middle of this battle between science and religion, and we must prepare to defend our collections from the influence of pro-creationist groups.

Steps to Defend Your Collection

Here's what you should do if your library finds itself caught in a predicament like ours.

Understand the controversy. We can't challenge something that we don't comprehend. So librarians need to fully understand the definition and implications of intelligent design theory. Don't just settle for what you read in the newspaper. Study what legitimate scientists and scientific journals have to say about this new generation of creationism.

Know your opposition. The intelligent design movement is led by a small group of calculating, well-organized, and well-financed activists based at the Discovery Institute's Center for Science and Culture in Seattle, WA. This think tank is attempting to insert its particular religious perspective into science education—as if it was science. By trying to give the prestigious label of "science" to its controversial theories, the group is misleading children and parents. Librarians and science teachers need to know that the battle against teaching evolution is not just a local issue—it's happening nationwide.

Contact the NCSE. The National Center for Science Education (www.ncseweb.org), a nonprofit organization, will give you the intellectual and moral support you need to successfully fight your battle. It provides information and materials that explain the intelligent design controversy and offers experienced, professional guidance. The center can also put you in touch with local experts, such as practicing scientists, science professors, and experts in scientific theory.

Plan your strategy. Identify the opposition's key points. Knowing the opposition's agenda can help you better respond to their arguments. We learned a lot about the donor's tactics and arguments by hearing him speak before the reconsideration committee.

Update your district's gift and selection policy. Following our experience, our district changed its gift policy and updated its selection criteria. Your board's policies should be periodically reviewed by you and your colleagues to ensure that they're relevant and up-to-date. If you don't have a selection or gift policy, ask a nearby district for guidance. Most districts are willing to share their policy statements.

Explain your policies before accepting gifts. To ensure that all donations are evaluated fairly, media specialists and administrators should be aware of their district's latest gift policies. Library support staff should refer all donations to the media specialist. Book donors need to know in advance that their gifts will be declined if they fail to meet the school's selection criteria or needs.

Respond to all charges of censorship. Your district's selection process will determine if a gift is formally accepted or rejected. Don't back down or change your mind if your decision reaches a reconsideration committee—this is the time to defend your professional integrity.

Organize wide-ranging support. Media specialists should not take on these monumental battles alone. It's critical to elicit the support of practicing scientists; experts on scientific theory; parents; teachers; religious leaders; and local, state, or national science organizations. Incorporating pseudo-science into a district's curriculum will only weaken the program and put students at a disadvantage when they enter college or the workforce.

Confront assaults on quality instruction and library resources. It may be easier for libraries to accept gifts rather than to upset a donor, but librarians should defend the process of selecting quality materials for their students and teachers.

8

Books That Address Sexuality Help Teens in Their Own Experiences

Isabel Kaplan

Isabel Kaplan is a novelist and a student at Harvard University.

A recent opinion piece by Wesley Scroggins in the Springfield (Missouri) News-Leader *illustrates the narrow-minded viewpoints behind efforts to ban books. Scoggins describes Laurie Halse Anderson's* Speak, *a sensitive novel about rape, as soft pornography. Anderson herself considers this charge horrific, since it implies that someone might actually find the rape of a fourteen-year-old girl sexually arousing. Equally problematic is the position of local school superintendent Vern Minor, who attempted to counter Scroggins's charges by pointing out that students are permitted to opt out of sex education classes, which in any case are abstinence-based. It would be wiser to allow students to opt out of math classes, which are far less likely to teach them anything that will prove important in shaping their futures; furthermore, the emphasis on abstinence simply ignores the reality that teenagers are likely to experiment with sex. Given the fact that many young victims of sexual assault have found comfort in the pages of* Speak, *it is imperative that those who care about intellectual freedom stand up to the Wesley Scrogginses of the world.*

Isabel Kaplan, "Why We Should Read 'Soft Pornography,'" *Huffington Post* (online), September 21, 2010. Copyright © 2010 by Isabel Kaplan. Reproduced by permission of the author.

Slaughterhouse-Five [by Kurt Vonnegut] has been removed from the English curriculum in a Missouri school district because of its inappropriateness. Score one for censorship. Speak, Laurie Halse Anderson's award-winning young adult novel about a teenager struggling with the aftermath of rape, has also come under attack for what one man calls the "soft pornography" aspect of the book. Score one for appalling judgment.

Wesley Scroggins, an Associate Professor at Missouri State University, . . . wrote an opinion piece for the Springfield News-Leader [in September, 2010] entitled "Filthy books demeaning to Republic education" in which he expresses outrage and concern at what's being taught in schools these days. Children are being forced to read books that are essentially "soft pornography," Scroggins says, and this needs to be stopped. The idea that Scroggins is equating Speak, a sensitive novel about rape, with pornography is horrendous. Is Scroggins suggesting that rape is somehow sexually exciting? I spoke with Laurie Halse Anderson via e-mail about her thoughts on the situation. Anderson says that she is "horrified. 'Pornographic' implies sexual excitement. Rape is not pornographic. Rape is assault, an attack. Anyone who finds the rape of a 14-year-old girl sexual exciting needs professional help. Scroggins completely mischaracterized the book. Speak explores the emotional aftermath of a rape victim, and follows her through her struggle to find the courage to speak up about what happened to her and reach for help."

Censorship Will Not Prevent Teens from Having Sex

The literary merits of Speak or Slaughterhouse-Five are apparently irrelevant. (How could a book have literary merit when it discusses such obscene things as sex? Right?) Or maybe the idea is that it's okay for novels to include sex scenes, just as long as we aren't letting young people read them. But Mr.

Scroggins, when has censorship ever been a good idea? Do you think that not informing students about sex will mean that they know nothing about it and therefore will abstain? Have you ever been a teenager? And while you do have the right to decide what your children read, who gave you the authority to decide what other people's children should and should not be allowed to read?

Scroggins' concerns . . . highlight a deeper and more troubling belief—that is, that young people should be prevented from exposure to anything that discusses sex and sexual activity in any way.

Republic [(Missouri) School District] Superintendent Vern Minor announced that *Slaughterhouse-Five* has been removed from the English curriculum. No word about *Speak*, but another book attacked by Scroggins, *Twenty Boy Summer* by Sarah Ockler, is currently under review regarding its status as a recommended book in a Republic school district library. The problem with *Twenty Boy Summer*, according to Scroggins, is that it depicts parties where teenagers get drunk, and "drunken teens also end up on the beach, where they use their condoms to have sex." Scroggins thinks children shouldn't be exposed to this kind of "immorality" because then they might go ahead and do some of the things depicted in the books. Like using their condoms to have sex. But wait, isn't encouraging teenagers to use condoms during sex a good message to send?

Not if you think teenagers should not be exposed to anything sex-related, I guess. Scroggins' concerns about *Slaughterhouse-Five*, *Speak*, and *Twenty Boy Summer* highlight a deeper and more troubling belief—that is, that young people should be prevented from exposure to anything that discusses sex and sexual activity in any way.

At the end of the article in the *Springfield News-Leader*, there is an Editor's Note saying that Superintendent Vern Minor pointed out that the curriculum is abstinence-based and students can opt-out of sex education classes.

Opt-out sex education classes? That's worse than having an opt-out option for Math class. No school board would ever approve opt-out Math, so why approve opt-out sex ed? Not knowing very much about geometry has less of a chance of shaping and inhibiting your future than becoming a mother at the age of sixteen does. And even if sex education classes were mandatory, abstinence based education is about as helpful and informative as teaching kids to do long division by counting on their fingers. Both are doable, but neither is very practical or plausible. Teenagers have sex. Not teaching them about how to practice safe sex only makes it more likely that they will practice unsafe sex.

[F]or me, far more important than sex ed was having the freedom to read without restrictions. When I was growing up, novels often helped me come to terms with and understand situations and questions that I was struggling with in my own life.

Novels Help Teens Cope with New Situations

I grew up in Los Angeles, and my sex education classes taught us all about reproduction, homosexuality, oral sex, and how to use a condom—all things that Scroggins mentions as being unfit topics of instruction for schools. But for me, far more important than sex ed was having the freedom to read without restrictions. When I was growing up, novels often helped me come to terms with and understand situations and questions that I was struggling with in my own life. As a writer, I am a firm believer in the power of words and the need for intellectual freedom. My first novel, *Hancock Park*, which is about a teenaged girl trying to make sense of her crazy Hollywood world, includes condoms and underaged drinking and discussions about sex. I'm fairly certain that Wesley Scroggins would not want to see it in school libraries. Needless to say, this is an issue I feel strongly about.

Speak has proven to have a tremendous impact on girls who have been sexually assaulted themselves—thousands of young women have written to Anderson about their own sexual assault experiences and the way that Anderson's novel gave them the courage to speak up. One girl wrote to Anderson saying, "I found *Speak* in the youth section of the public library when I was in 7th grade. I had experienced sexual assault and I was a cutter, and I had walled myself off so much not much could reach me. But this book did, I was grateful for the honesty and a voice besides my own to say the things I was feeling, things too scary to tell my mother or my friends. And considering the situation outside of myself, gave me perspective to see *me* beyond that pain." Without *Speak*, this girl, and countless others, would not have had the courage to come forward about their sexual assaults. How could censoring Anderson's book (or any other book, for that matter) possibly be a good idea?

Speak has proven to have a tremendous impact on girls who have been sexually assaulted themselves . . .

When asked about the state of book censorship in the U.S. today, Anderson said, "censorship attempts are on the increase. But the ability of people willing to defend intellectual freedom is developing exponentially. I am confident we will prevail."

In order to prevail, it's up to those of us who care about intellectual freedom to stand up and protest cases like this Missouri school district situation and make sure that the Wesley Scroggins of the world have no chance to make ignorant and harmful decisions for their communities.

9

Books on Violence and Bullying Can Help Teens Develop Empathy

Michael Cart

Michael Cart is an educator and authority on young adult literature, a reviewer for Booklist *magazine, and the author of numerous published works, including* Young Adult Literature: From Romance to Realism.

Risky behaviors, including physical and emotional violence, substance abuse, and unsafe sex, are very real factors in the lives of twenty-first century teenagers, who find themselves in a world dominated by violence both real (such as the 1999 Columbine High School shootings) and imagined (such as rap music, video games, and other forms of media). In such an environment, it might seem counterintuitive to maintain that students need more, not less, material addressing issues of violence honestly and realistically, but this is in fact the case. In contrast to electronic media, literature has the advantage of helping readers experience empathy and sympathy. A wide variety of recent books for young readers offer helpful approaches to bullying, an increasingly prevalent concern on grade-school campuses in the United States. Among the responses to bullying addressed in such works are the outer-directed violence employed by school shooters, the inner-directed violence of self-mutilation and suicide, and the creative nonviolent approach in James Howe's The Misfits, *which inspired a national No Name Calling Week. Of par-*

ticular concern is the growing practice of cyberbullying, which offers a number of advantages to bullies and disadvantages to their victims.

Risky behaviors remain very real factors in the daily lives of 21st-century teens. Ranging from physical and emotional violence to drug and alcohol abuse, from risky sexual practices resulting in STDs [sexually transmitted diseases] and unintended pregnancies to driving recklessly and carrying weapons to school, these behaviors make up the main threat to adolescents' health, according to the National Longitudinal Study on Adolescent Health.

While the incidence of specific behaviors may wax and wane like the moon, one thing remains constant: "You have to realize that all adolescents are going to take risks," asserts Lynn Ponton, author of *The Romance of Risk: Why Teenagers Do the Things They Do.* "Adolescents define themselves," she said in a May 10, 1999, *New York Times* article, "through rebellion and anger at parents or other adults, engaging in high-risk behaviors including drinking, smoking, drug use, reckless driving, unsafe sexual activity, disordered eating, self-mutilation, stealing, gang activity, and violence."

"You have to realize that all adolescents are going to take risks."

The riskiest of teen behaviors involves violence and the resulting injuries that remain the leading causes of death among all youth aged 5–19. Of these deaths, 67% result from injury, 16% from homicide, and 14% from suicide, according to the Centers for Disease Control [CDC]. These are startling—and sometimes shattering—statistics. The CDC reports that "a number of factors can increase the risk of a youth engaging in violence." Among them: "a prior history of violence; drug, alcohol, or tobacco use; poor family functioning; poor grades in school; poverty in the community; and association with delinquent peers."

Violence Is Prevalent in Young People's Lives

It is hard not to think that some impact comes from growing up in a violence-ridden world—the real thing, as in the [1995] Oklahoma City bombing, the [1999] Columbine [High School] shootings, 9/11, international terrorism, and the wars in Iraq and Afghanistan, as well as the imagined but powerfully visualized (and sometimes glamorized) violence in movies, on TV, on the Internet, and in video games (Grand Theft Auto, anyone?). Indeed, according to the University of Michigan Health System, "Literally thousands of studies since the 1950s have asked whether there is a link between exposure to media violence and violent behavior. All but 18 have answered 'Yes.'"

Accordingly, the exponential growth of a media presence in adolescent lives may give one pause. In his fascinating 2008 book *Guyland: The Perilous World Where Boys Become Men*, sociologist Michael Kimmel writes, "Today's young people— from little kids to adults in their late 20s and early 30s— represent the most technologically sophisticated and media savvy generation in our history. The average American home . . . has three TVs, two VCRs, three radios, two tape players, two CD players, more than one video game console, and more than one computer. . . . American kids 8 to 18 spend about seven hours a day interacting with some form of electronic media; the average 13-to-18-year-old spends two hours a day just playing video games."

Kimmel, who teaches at Stony Brook (N.Y.) University, chillingly continues, "The dominant emotion in all these forms of entertainment is anger. From violent computer games to extreme sports, from racist and misogynistic radio show content to furious rap and heavy metal music, from the X-rated to the Xbox, the amount of rage and sensory violence to which guys have become accustomed is overwhelming. It doesn't even occur to them that all this media consumption might be extreme." Extreme and extremely desensitizing and ultimately dehumanizing, perhaps?

The American Academy of Pediatrics agrees, pointing out that "Extensive research evidence indicates that media violence can contribute to aggressive behavior, desensitization to violence, nightmares, and fear of being harmed."

In the wake of the tsunami of violence inundating today's YAs [young adults], do we really need books that embrace violence, too?

As we have seen, young people have good reason to fear being harmed, and it doesn't help that, as Kimmel notes, "The most avid consumers of this new media . . . are young men 16 to 26. It's the demographic group most prized by advertisers," who, needless to say, cheerfully stoke the fires of that young male avidity.

Books Allow Teens to Experience Violence in a Different Way

Does it seem counterintuitive to now argue that we need more—not less—literature that addresses these same issues honestly and realistically? In the wake of the tsunami of violence inundating today's YAs [young adults], do we really need books that embrace violence, too? Well, yes, I believe we do.

After all, the great gift literature can give its readers that new—and old—media can't is the experience of empathy and sympathy. Books can take their readers into the interior lives of characters in ways that television and video can't. They can not only show what is happening to characters but also powerfully convey how what is happening feels. Interactive games and media can, doubtless, improve hand-to-eye coordination. But books can improve heart-to-eye coordination and even, I would argue, create it when—as increasingly seems to be the case—it is altogether absent.

The shocking absence of empathy in today's adolescent lives is nowhere more powerfully evidenced than in the epidemic of bullying that is plaguing America's schools, playgrounds, parks, and neighborhoods.

The New Spotlight on Bullying

Bullying is hardly new, but the freshly minted attention it has been given increased dramatically in the wake of the Columbine High School shootings. Indeed, the CDC reports that an estimated 30% of all kids between the 6th and 10th grades (i.e., 5.7 million-plus) now report being involved in bullying.

If any good thing came out of the Columbine tragedy, it was the elevation of attention given to this epidemic and the very rapid emergence of a subgenre of young adult literature that continues to explore the many aspects of this issue with insight and, yes, empathy. Arguably the first book to emerge in this category was Todd Strasser's chilling documentary novel *Give a Boy a Gun*. In it Strasser charts the growing disaffection of two teenage boys, Gary and Brendan, who first dream of taking revenge on the people who have bullied them and then transform that dream into reality.

A number of other novels dealing with school violence have appeared in the decade since Strasser's; among them are Ron Koertge's verse novel *The Brimstone Journals*, Nancy Garden's *Endgame*, Diane Tullson's *Lockdown*, C.G. Watson's *Quad*, and Jennifer Brown's *Hate List*.

Not all violent responses to bullying are directed at the bullies; sometimes the target is the victim him- or, more often, herself. One of the most common ways that teen girls punish themselves for being different is by cutting. Shelley Stoehr's 1991 novel *Crosses* is the first YA novel to examine this growing phenomenon, which has since become a fixture in teen fiction. Another gravely misguided strategy for coping with bullying is suicide, a topic that was taboo in YA literature for many years (for fear of creating a copycat effect among young readers). This has recently begun to change, since the enormous success of Jay Asher's 2007 novel *Thirteen Reasons Why*, in which a teenage girl named Hannah kills herself, leaving a package of audiocassettes articulating her reasons. Laurie Halse Anderson also addresses this issue in *Twisted*, in which a teen boy contemplates killing himself in response to intolerable bullying.

Clearly Howe's novel [The Misfits] *touched a nerve; its huge popularity has inspired a national No Name Calling Week that is observed by middle and elementary schools all across the country.*

Fortunately, not all bullying results in apocalyptic violence. Arguably the best-known book on how the targets of bullying can find a creative way to respond is James Howe's *The Misfits*, the story of four middle school students who are, yes, misfits and are accordingly the targets of painful bullying. Instead of getting even, the four resolve to change their school's climate of abuse by running for class office on a no-name-calling platform. Clearly Howe's novel touched a nerve; its huge popularity has inspired a national No Name Calling Week that is observed by middle and elementary schools all across the country.

Cyberbullying Is on the Rise

Bullying is not a uniquely American problem, of course. Indeed, the newest kind of bullying has international ramifications thanks to the ubiquity of the internet. I'm referring here, of course, to cyberbullying: the posting of innuendo, put-downs, gossip, lies, and—perhaps worst of all—compromising photos online.

"Cyberbullying is the fastest-growing form of bullying happening around the world," observed C.J. Bott, author of two books about the subject, in the June 2008 VOYA [*Voice of Youth Advocates* magazine]. One of the attractions of this technique is that it allows the bully both anonymity and the ability to inflict pain without being forced to see its effect, which an August 26, 2004, *New York Times* article noted "also seems to incite a deeper level of meanness." Perhaps worst of all, there is no escaping this type of bullying; it spreads virally and follows the victim everywhere. Cyberbullies can be both boys and girls, but the latter tend to predominate. A few recent books about this invidious phenomenon are Laura Ruby's *Good Girls* and Shana Norris's *Something to Blog About*. Perhaps because of these books, a new anti-bullying technique has begun gaining favor. In an April 5, 2009, front-page article in the *New York Times*, reporter Winnie Hu wrote, "The emphasis on empathy here and in schools nationwide is the latest front in a decade-long campaign against bullying and violence." According to Hu, "the Character Education Partnership, a nonprofit group in Washington, said 18 states—including New York, Florida, Illinois, Nebraska, and California—require programs to foster core values such as empathy, respect, responsibility, and integrity."

Violent Books Promote Empathy and Hope

Not all violence is related to bullying, of course. On September 11, 2001—scarcely two years after Columbine—the attack on Manhattan's World Trade Center and the Pentagon brought the specter of international terrorism—and the threat of violent death—into the forefront of American teens' consciousness. Within a year a dozen or more books, virtually all of them nonfiction, had appeared with the goal of helping young readers of all ages to cope with this new fear factor in their lives. Although short fiction was included in *911: The Book of Help*, the anthology that Marc Aronson, Marianne Carus, and I coedited, full-length fiction about this terrible event has been slower to surface. Joyce Maynard's crossover novel *The Usual Rules* appeared in 2003, and Francine Prose's YA title *Bullyville* followed in 2007. Finally, in 2009, David Levithan's *Love Is the Higher Law* appeared.

In an eloquent letter to the reader, Levithan explained his reasons for taking us back to that terrible event: "As time goes by, it's really easy to remember 9/11 and the days afterward as a time of tragedy, fear, grief, and loss. Less easy to remember—and even harder to convey—is that it was amazing not just for the depth of that loss, but also for the heights of humanity that occurred. The kindness. The feeling of community. The deepening of love and friendship."

This, it seems to me, is the most compelling argument one can offer for writing fiction about even the most unpleasant realities of teens' lives. For life, even at its darkest, can hold the promise of hope and positive change—especially when we read about it with open minds and hearts, with intellectual attention and emotional empathy.

10

Mein Kampf Should Be Published, Not Banned

Ben Macintyre

Ben Macintyre is a British historian and columnist.

Shortly before its publication in England in October 1933, Adolf Hitler's Mein Kampf *appeared in a serialized version on the pages of the London* Times. *First published in German in 1924,* Mein Kampf *("My Struggle") is purportedly Hitler's autobiography, but it actually constitutes a Nazi manifesto and a blueprint for the atrocities that followed Hitler's accession to power in 1933. Not only is it an evil book; it is also poorly written. Yet* Times *editor George Dawson was right to expose readers to it. William L. Shirer, a leading authority on the Third Reich, suggested that if more people had known what Hitler intended to do, they might have made more of an effort to stop him. Today* Mein Kampf *is banned in many countries, including Germany, where its underground status gives it a certain cache among neo-Nazis and others sympathetic to Hitler's views. In advance of the 2015 expiration of its German copyright, publishers would be wise to begin preparing a cheap, scholarly, annotated version with critical commentary for German readers.*

Seventy-four years ago this week [July 27, 2007], The *Times* started serialising the worst book ever written. Adolf Hitler had dictated *Mein Kampf* in Landsburg Prison in 1924, while incarcerated for his attempted putsch [coup] against the Ger-

Ben Macintyre, "Publish and Debunk This Relic of History," *Times* (London), July 27, 2007. Copyright © 2007 by NEWS INTERNATIONAL SYNDICATION. Reproduced by permission.

man Government. The book would not be published in Britain until October 1933, but this newspaper obtained the rights to run exclusive extracts four months earlier.

The *Times* explained that it was publishing this vile, anti-Semitic rant on the grounds that "readers will find it illuminating as a psychological revelation [which] will show how Hitler came to hate the Jews". Even so, the editor of the day, George Dawson, was plainly holding his nose as he placed *Mein Kampf* ("My Struggle") in the public domain.

Are there some words so ugly in import and so violent in intent, that they should be locked away?

The accompanying editorial spoke of the author as a "fanatical anti-Semite" with "a few ideas, harshly created and stubbornly held". It noted Hitler's "revengeful fury" and the "cruel acts of savagery which have degraded Germany in the eyes of the world". The editorial concluded: "The Hitler regime has actually been established by violence [and] legalised terrorism is still necessary to its maintenance."

People Have Always Questioned the Decision to Publish *Mein Kampf*

Few in 1933 could have foreseen the full scale of the horror that Hitler would shortly unleash, but there is a flicker of premonition in this newspaper's palpable distaste. Dawson must also have wondered whether, in giving space to Hitler's noxious ideas, he was also spreading and encouraging them. Was the *Times* justified in publishing Hitler's tract? Or are there some words so ugly in import and so violent in intent, that they should be locked away? Is Hitler's creed an ideological poison, liable to corrupt and contaminate anyone who is exposed to it? These questions have been asked about *Mein Kampf* ever since it first appeared, and it is an issue of fierce debate in Germany today, where Horst Möller, a leading German historian, has called for the book to be published openly for the first time since 1945.

The Bavarian state authorities own the copyright to Hitler's writings, but maintain an effective ban by refusing all requests to print it. Officially, the book cannot be bought in Germany, Israel, Norway or Switzerland. It is illegal to own it in Austria and to sell it in the Netherlands. But the book is available for sale in the US and Britain, as well as through internet bookshops. About 3,000 copies are sold every year in the UK.

The Text Exposes Hitler's Weakness

Mein Kampf is the central defining text of racial hatred, a lurid, paranoid diatribe founded on the lie of Aryan supremacy. It is not only evil but amazingly badly written, being repetitious, anti-factual, rambling and turgid, the testimony of a furious, self-pitying failure with a slender grasp on reality and none whatever on grammar. It was a huge bestseller: each newly married couple, graduating student, and soldier at the front was presented with a copy by the Third Reich; Hitler earned more than $1 million a year in royalties. It is wicked rubbish, at once stomach-turning and soporific [dull]; everyone should read it, once.

Holocaust survivors are understandably unhappy at the prospect of a book that caused such bloodshed becoming freely available once more in the country that gave birth to Nazism. Yet whatever sympathy one may feel for those who suffered, no book should be banned, however pernicious. Allowed to fester in the dark corners of neo-Nazism, Hitler's ideas continue to hold a spurious glamour for the twisted few: held up to the light, they shrivel, in treating this disease, exposure to fresh air is always more effective than quarantine.

Some argued as much from the beginning. William L. Shirer, the American journalist and historian who covered the rise of the Third Reich, suggested that if Hitler's ideas had been more widely disseminated and understood outside Germany in the 1930s, then the world might have taken action in time to stop him.

The *Times* was right to publish extracts from *Mein Kampf* in 1933; the publisher Hutchinson was brave and right to issue a cheap wartime edition in order that British people might better understand what we were fighting for, and against. And Mr Möller is surely right to argue that Germany has now left the spectre of Nazism so far behind, that it can trust itself to read Hitler's creed without fear of reinfection.

A New Edition of *Mein Kampf* Will Take Away Its Mystique and Power

Quite apart from the issue of free speech, there is the practical consideration that book-banning is virtually impossible in the internet age. The Nazis themselves tried, and failed, to ban and burn the "degenerate" books they feared, and in the process lent those works underground status. Today any neo-Nazi with half a brain (rather more than the usual complement), can download *Mein Kampf* and feel aggrieved and special for having to do so in secret.

Allowed to fester in the dark corners of neo-Nazism, Hitler's ideas continue to hold a spurious glamour for the twisted few: held up to the light, they shrivel.

The copyright of *Mein Kampf* in Germany will expire in 2015, and then German publishers will be free to publish it. How much better, then, to produce a cheap, scholarly, annotated version in German now, with a commentary comprehensively debunking it. That would be a mark of moral courage, a demonstration that Germany has come to terms with its past and can look on the evil of Nazism with confident disdain instead of a lingering fear.

Mein Kampf is a historical relic that has retained its power to horrify: it should be preserved and exhibited in the same way as Auschwitz, the killing fields of Cambodia and Holocaust museums everywhere. Germany has struggled to explore and understand its own history with an honesty that stands as a beacon to other traumatised nations, from South Africa to Iraq to Northern Ireland. Hitler's apologia for mass murder is a painful but necessary part of that story. It should be published, and damned.

11

Hateful Texts Are Dangerous Even When Exposed as Propaganda

Marilyn Henry

Marilyn Henry, was managing editor of Judaism: A Quarterly Journal of Jewish Life and Thought *until her passing in March 2011. She also wrote several books on modern Jewish history.*

As the 2015 expiration of the German copyright on Mein Kampf *approaches, the question of what to do about Adolf Hitler's infamous racist diatribe has been the topic of much discussion in Germany. Historian Horst Moeller calls for the preemptive publication of a scholarly annotated version with footnotes debunking Hitler's spurious claims. Moeller's position, however, is not supported by the experience of the second-most notorious work of anti-Semitic "literature." First published in Russia in 1903,* The Protocols of the Learned Elders of Zion *presents an alleged Jewish plan for world domination. Although it has long since been exposed as a forgery, interest in the* Protocols *remains high. Jews should be able to counter its lies, but they are mostly ignorant of the book's message. Hadassa Ben-Itto has helped increase awareness of the* Protocols *with her book* The Lie That Wouldn't Die: The Protocols of the Elders of Zion *(2005). Nevertheless, many still regard the tract as legitimate and continue to believe its claims of a global Jewish conspiracy.*

Marilyn Henry, "The Peril in Ignoring the Protocols," *Judaism: A Quarterly Journal of Jewish Life and Thought*, vol. 55, no. 3–4 (Fall–Winter 2006). Reprinted by permission of Judaism: The Journal of Jewish Life & Thought and the American Jewish Congress.

There is much commotion in Germany these days [2006] about what to do about *Mein Kampf*, Adolf Hitler's hate-filled rantings from jail. The fear is that when the copyright expires in 2015, the possible mass publication of the book would introduce new generations to Hitler's odious views and traumatize the remaining survivors of the Holocaust.

A German historian, Horst Moeller, has called for a sort of pre-emptive measure. Moeller, director of the Institute of Contemporary History in Munich, suggests that an annotated edition of the book be published before the copyright expires. He apparently believes that a version of the book with footnotes refuting Hitler's views would somehow deflate them.

Can Scholarship Neutralize a Racist Text?

Sadly, there is no evidence that such debunking works. Take the invidious book *The Protocols of the Learned Elders of Zion*. The enduring tract is labeled as the minutes of meetings of the so-called "Elders of Zion," a Jewish criminal conspiracy to dominate the world. It has been exposed as a libel, a fraud, a plagiarism. We can debunk it until we are blue in the face. Called the greatest hoax of the century, it survived for so long and generated so much hatred that it comes with a warning, a "special note" from Amazon.com, the world's most recognizable bookseller. "This book is one of the most infamous, and tragically influential, examples of racist propaganda ever written. It may be useful to some as a tool in the teaching of the history of anti-Semitism, but it's unquestionably propaganda," the bookseller says on its website.

Not everyone who has sold the book has gone this far. In fact, in one of the most notable examples of the opposite approach, Wal-Mart's website reportedly carried the following:

> Some say the issue has already been settled conclusively—that it is clearly a forgery. Although there may be final evidence to this effect, we have not seen a clear and convincing version of it produced by those making the claim . . .

If, however, The Protocols are genuine (which can never be proven conclusively), it might cause some of us to keep a wary eye on world affairs.

For its part, Amazon.com, which classifies the book as "controversial knowledge" (apparently along with books on UFOs [unidentified flying objects], demonic possession and "all manner of conspiracy theories"), also uses this as a marketing opportunity for books that expose the Protocols.

Among these are *The Plot: The Secret Story of the Protocols of the Elders of Zion* by the late graphic artist Will Eisner and *The Lie That Wouldn't Die: The Protocols of the Elders of Zion*, by Hadassa Ben-Itto.

[T]here has been a fundamental Jewish ignorance, if not willful blindness, about the book [The Protocols].

Eisner's book requires an enormous level of sophistication and appreciation of irony from its readers. Ben-Itto's work is a literary and historical gem. An authority on human rights, a former Israeli representative at the United Nations [U.N.] and a veteran Israeli judge, Ben-Itto retired from the judicial life to research and write an authoritative account of the life the Protocols.

Even Patent Untruths Cannot Be Ignored

The Lie That Wouldn't Die reads, in part, like a legal drama and a historical thriller, in which Ben-Itto explains "how the greatest hoax of the century survived for so long and generated so much hatred."

She also bravely acknowledges that there has been a fundamental Jewish ignorance, if not willful blindness, about the book. Jews know of the Protocols. We know that this notorious forgery is powerful propaganda used to disseminate dangerous myths that are accepted as truths and used to foment anti-Semitism. We know; others apparently do not. As Ben-Itto points out, she represented Israel at the U.N. General Assembly where people quoted the Protocols, but Ben-Itto did not use the opportunity to dispute them. She had not read them, because, as she notes, Jews did not read the Protocols. Instead, they are dismissed with contempt and unworthy of being dignified with a comment.

This was a mistake. Ben-Itto believes Jews ignore the Protocols at great risk. Everyone else seems to have access to them. When she began her quest for the truth of the Protocols, they already had been translated into nearly every language—except Hebrew.

Her book intersperses personal reflections about her quest with the stories of the people and the proceedings over a century and various continents that attempted to perpetuate and to destroy the lie. "I had set out to investigate the story behind a book, but as I did so, a procession of people started crowding into the story, forcing themselves upon me. These men and a surprising number of women have all played a part in the saga," she wrote. "The story of the book, I soon discovered, would become the story of the people who had inspired, created, distributed and exploited it, as well as those who had finally exposed it."

Repeated often enough, vile accusations filter into the public consciousness, shape public opinion and sentiment, and often are mistaken for fact.

Ben-Itto also highlights the role of the book in a significant shift in the nature of anti-Semitism, from a religiously based phenomenon to a political one. In a trial in the early 1930s in Bern, Switzerland, Georges Brunschvig, a young lawyer, represented the Jewish community in a suit against the Nazi publishers of the Protocols. Among Brunschvig's tasks was how "to explain to the Swiss judge how, instead of traditional religious anti-Semitism that vilified the Jews as Christ-killers, there now existed a form of political anti-Semitism, based on the so-called Jewish conspiracy theory, which depicted the Jews as the greatest danger to world order."

Even Though They Have Been Exposed as a Forgery, the Protocols Retain Their Power

Although Ben-Itto's work is not first to challenge the Protocols, her documentation and accounts of successful legal proceedings are credited with firmly establishing that the Protocols are a forgery and are used with insidious intent. The book also was published in Russia, where the media reported on the Protocols as deception.

On one hand, it is cause for celebration. Repeated often enough, vile accusations filter into the public consciousness, shape public opinion and sentiment, and often are mistaken for fact. They must be challenged. As a friendly Latin American diplomat reminded Ben-Itto at the U.N. decades ago: "You Jews should have learned that lesson. You ignored Hitler's *Mein Kampf* at your peril." To ignore the Protocols is dangerous.

Facts and figures about forgeries and hoaxes will not diminish a widely held view of the Jewish conspiracy to rule the world.

We should not overstate the impact of challenging the Protocols, however. They are for sale. Despicable though the book is, banning it runs counter to free speech and smacks of Nazi book burning.

As important as Ben-Itto's book is, it reminds us of another book that would not die. This is the book that explains it, but will not slay it. Facts and figures about forgeries and hoaxes will not diminish a widely held view of the Jewish conspiracy to rule the world. That is a sentiment, an attitude, that is not based on intellect or reason and that cannot be discredited by documentation and other evidence, much like Moeller's idea for annotating *Mein Kampf*, as if that would undercut its racist authority.

What Ben-Itto writes of a historical character in her book remains true. We know "from bitter experience it was fruitless to confront the anti-Semites in the so-called marketplace of ideas. This was not about ideas, it was about prejudice."

12

Expensive Libel Lawsuits Can Indirectly Lead to Censorship

Laura Miller

Laura Miller is a frequent contributor to the New York Times Book Review *and other print and electronic publications, including Salon.com, which she cofounded in 1995.*

Book banning is not the only form of censorship; another is the use of costly libel suits such as the one filed by Texas developer H. Walker Royall against Carla Main for her exposé Bulldozed. *Even more serious are the challenges presented under British libel law. The latter so heavily favors the plaintiff that many rich and powerful litigants have employed "libel tourism," the practice of suing in British courts to settle cases that would never get a hearing under the much broader free-speech protections of US law. A British lawsuit by Saudi billionaire Khalid bin Mahfouz against American author Rachel Ehrenfeld for her book* Funding Evil *prompted the passage of House Resolution 2765, which President Obama signed into law. Known as the SPEECH (Securing the Protection of Our Enduring and Established Constitutional Heritage) Act, the law prohibits federal enforcement of foreign libel rulings that do not meet the standards of US libel law. Awareness of the impact libel cases can have on free speech is important for all who support intellectual freedom; even if lawsuits fail, they may prove costly enough to prevent the publication of material that may risk legal action from plaintiffs with deep pockets.*

Last week [September 25–October 2, 2010] was Banned Books Week, a worthy institution calling attention to efforts to remove books from public libraries and school curricula. This annual event has become so successful that, although the American Library Association reported "460 recorded attempts to remove materials from libraries in 2009," a close examination suggests that many of these amounted to mere "challenges"—written objections submitted to librarians or teachers by isolated crackpots or control freak parents with minimal chances of seeing their censorious desires fulfilled.

Landmark Defamation Case in Texas

But book banning isn't the only form censorship takes, and schools and libraries aren't the only places where it happens. As reported in *Publishers Weekly* [*P.W.*], the Texas Appeals Court last week heard an important but little-known case filed against Carla Main, author of *Bulldozed: "Kelo," Eminent Domain and the American Lust for Land,* and her publisher, the conservative press Encounter Books. The plaintiff, developer H. Walker Royall, claims that Main has defamed him and wants her book yanked off the market and any future printings curtailed. Royall has also attempted to sue a newspaper that reviewed the book and even a law professor who provided a back-cover endorsement. (The latter case has already been dismissed.)

Main's book describes a long-standing and rancorous dispute over eminent domain seizures in the town of Freeport, Texas, and her defense is spearheaded by the Texas-based Institute for Justice, which describes itself as the "nation's only libertarian public interest law firm." While Main's plight may not tug as forcefully on the heartstrings as the idea of young people deprived of the right to read by fundamentalist fanatics, she and her publisher are nevertheless fighting an important battle.

At issue is whether, in Texas, books are entitled to the same First Amendment protections as "news" organizations. If the appeals court agrees that they are, the case will be prevented from proceeding to litigation, saving Main and her publisher from further legal expenses. According to *P.W.*, Main's brief states that Royall doesn't contest the facts as she reports them, but objects to how she "characterizes the project and Royall's involvement." And while it may seem unlikely that he could ever prevail against her, chances are the costs of defending *Bulldozed* have by now far exceeded any income the book may have earned.

[E]ven baseless libel actions can end up suppressing speech.

For a glimpse of how even baseless libel actions can end up suppressing speech, we have only to look at an article former publisher Dan Hind wrote for the *Guardian* last month. Hind edited the British editions of Eric Schlosser's *Fast Food Nation,* Greg Palast's *The Best Democracy Money Can Buy* and Misha Glenny's *McMafia,* among other important works of book-length investigative journalism.

British Libel Law Invites "Libel Tourism"

British libel law is notoriously harsh—so much so that when asked to contemplate the possibility of Facebook founder Mark Zuckerberg suing the makers of the film *The Social Network* for misrepresenting him, First Amendment lawyer Floyd Abrams told the *New York Times*, "He ought to sue in London, where the law is so very pro plaintiff and so very indifferent to what we consider to be free speech rights."

Abrams was being sardonic, but not fanciful. The practice he describes is called libel tourism, and it's been employed by the wealthy and powerful to stifle critics even when the critics' books weren't published in England. Saudi billionaire Sheikh

Khalid bin Mahfouz used a British court to sue American author Rachel Ehrenfeld for libeling him in her book *Funding Evil*, on the grounds that 23 copies of her book were sold in the U.K. via the Internet. Ehrenfeld, who refused to participate in the trial, was ordered to pay a 10,000-pound default judgment by the court.

British libel law often makes the publication of books on current affairs prohibitively expensive.

Ehrenfeld's experience prompted the passage of anti-libel-tourism legislation on the state level, as well as the SPEECH Act (H.R. 2765), signed into law by President Obama in August. The new law prevents federal enforcement of foreign libel judgments in the U.S. if those judgments do not meet the tougher standards for libel here. However, it can't do much to help American authors and publishers with assets in the U.K., let alone British writers and publishers.

Strict Libel Laws May Intimidate Publishers and Writers

As Hind describes it, British libel law often makes the publication of books on current affairs prohibitively expensive. Even before the book is published, it must be exhaustively vetted by lawyers. (Vetting happens in the U.S. as well, of course, but it doesn't have to be anywhere near as rigorous.) While in the U.S. the burden of proof for libel is on the plaintiff (who must demonstrate that the defendant willfully made false statements with malicious intent), in the U.K., it's up to the defendant to demonstrate, using the sworn testimony of primary sources, that his or her claims are true. If you'd talked to Erie Schlosser about the misdeeds of your fast-food-company employer or given Misha Glenny important information about international organized crime, how would you feel about that? "The game," Hind writes, "is rigged to make it all but impossible to say anything substantial about any powerful individual or institution without running eye-watering risks."

There's no more effective way to ban a book than to prevent it from being written in the first place.

Even when a libel case is almost certain to fail, defending a book and its author in court is costly. As a result, according to Hind, British publishers hesitate to take on books that seem likely to attract such suits, and in turn, writers hesitate, or are simply unable, to write them.

Banned Books Week has been such a success at calling attention to targeted books that in quite a few instances it has won them a wider circle of readers. As crucial as it is to continue to protect those books from would-be censors, we should be paying equal attention to any encroachment of libel and defamation litigation on authors' freedom to criticize people rich and powerful enough to dispatch a pack of lawyers at will. There's no more effective way to ban a book than to prevent it from being written in the first place.

13

Financial Risks of Libel Suits Overstate the Limits on Free Speech

David Engel

David Engel is a partner at the British law firm of Addleshaw Goddard.

Jo Glanville, editor of the magazine Index on Censorship, *describes British libel law as "a malign force" that stifles free speech, but libel laws are both necessary and, in the case of Britain, far less restrictive than Glanville claims. British libel law gives individuals and companies the right to protect their reputations against unjustifiable damage; therefore, if the claims made in a published work are justifiable, authors and publishers have nothing to fear. Glanville maintains that "no win, no fee" conditional fee agreements make it too easy for plaintiffs to bring libel suits, because they do not have to pay any lawyer fees unless they win. In reality, however, most law firms operate on a "no win, low fee" basis: the plaintiff's lawyer fees are discounted if the case is unsuccessful, but the plaintiff must still assume some financial risk in bringing the suit. Furthermore, if an author or publisher is willing to correct and apologize for demonstrably false statements at the outset, most plaintiffs will not pursue extensive financial damages. Most publishers carry libel insurance, but if they do not want to incur this cost—or the risk of a court case— they should choose more carefully the material they publish.*

Jo Glanville of *Index on Censorship* complains that Britain's libel laws are "a malign force" and "the most significant daily chill on free speech in the UK". I would respectfully disagree.

Freedom of speech is not, whether in the UK or anywhere else, an unfettered right. There are sound philosophical and jurisprudential reasons why that has always been the case, and why it should continue to be the case. Most people would agree that in a democratic society it is not desirable for people to be free, for example, to incite mass murder. Similarly, the right to freedom of speech has always been constrained by other rights, such as the law of copyright (designed to reward and therefore encourage creative effort) and the rights to reputation and to confidentiality.

[T]he right to freedom of speech has always been constrained by other rights, such as the law of copyright ... and the rights to reputation and to confidentiality.

Libel Laws Protect People's Reputations and Privacy

The European convention on human rights, which *Index on Censorship* would presumably support, neatly encapsulates this balancing exercise, according the citizens of signatory states a right to freedom of expression (article 10), but only provided that the exercise of such a right does not unnecessarily impact upon a countervailing right to privacy and to reputation (article 8).

Britain's libel laws are the means by which individuals and companies can protect their reputations from being unjustifiably damaged, whether by the media or by the NGOs [nongovernmental organizations] referred to by Glanville. The key word is unjustifiably. Where the media or a campaigning organisation is justified in trashing a company's or individual's reputation, they are perfectly entitled to do so and there is nothing in Britain's libel laws to prevent them.

Fee Agreements Do Not Reward Frivolous Claims

Glanville says that "the key issue is costs" and that "the use of 'no win no fee' CFAs (conditional fee agreements [an agreement whereby the lawyer only gets paid if his or her client wins the case]) has turned libel courts into casinos".

First, and leaving aside the fact that awards of damages in the libel courts have in truth decreased markedly over the last 20 or so years, it is incorrect to assume that CFAs are necessarily "no win, no fee" with a 100% uplift in the event of success.

Libel—and other—lawyers can and do act on a "no win, low fee" basis. The client receives a discount on the standard charging rate if the claim is unsuccessful, but that discount is most unlikely to exceed 50%. In other words, the risk is shared by client and lawyer. Likewise, any uplift in the event of success is calculated, in accordance with Law Society guidelines, to reflect the risk taken on and is highly unlikely to be anywhere near 100%. The stronger the claim (and therefore the lower the risk for the lawyers), the lower the uplift for success.

This is a model that is fair to all parties and strikes a proper and equitable balance between affording access to justice and maintaining any costs uplift at a sensible and proportionate level.

For Libel Claimants, Financial Compensation Is Secondary

Second, to accuse CFAs of having a "chilling effect" on freedom of speech simply does not reflect the commercial realities. A potential claimant who does not have at least a reasonable case is highly unlikely to be able to persuade any law firm to act on a CFA whether "no win, no fee" or otherwise. In any event, all that most claimants want is an acknowledgement from the newspaper or book publisher in question that they got it wrong and are willing to apologise. If they do so at the outset, the legal costs will be minimal and the claimant is unlikely to press for substantial damages. Nobody will be put out of business.

A claim in libel is not primarily a claim for financial compensation. It is about protecting the claimant's reputation. It is therefore simplistic to seek to compare the level of costs with the amount of damages recovered.

[A]ll that most claimants want is an acknowledgement from the newspaper or book publisher in question that they got it wrong and are willing to apologise.

Publishers Need Not Be Constrained by Fear of Libel Suits

Equally, if the publisher is on strong ground there is no reason why "faced with a lawyer's letter, most publishers have to surrender if they want to stay in business". The costs-shifting principle in English litigation (where the loser must pay most of the winner's legal costs) ensures precisely the opposite. The only reason a publisher would surrender on receipt of a letter of complaint would be if it was likely to lose any legal proceedings that followed. And it would only lose if it should not have published the offending material in the first place.

In addition, most publishers will themselves carry libel insurance to cover precisely this financial exposure. If they choose not to incur the premiums required to maintain such cover, then it is always open to them to take more care about the material they publish.

The media, and other publishers, may not like the fact that CFAs have put ordinary mortals on a more equal financial footing with them in pursuing complaints. But to describe this as a threat to freedom of expression is unreal.

14

E-Books Are Vulnerable
to Digital Banning

Farhad Manjoo

Farhad Manjoo is a technology columnist for Slate *and author of* True Enough: Learning to Live in a Post-Fact Society.

In July 2009 the Internet retailer Amazon.com remotely deleted what it maintained were illegal copies of George Orwell's novels Nineteen Eighty-Four *and* Animal Farm *from customers' Kindle e-readers. Although the company targeted bootlegged copies of other works, the fact that both books depict thought control in totalitarian societies made this incident particularly noteworthy. Electronic technology has changed the rules of information ownership: Amazon, Apple, and other companies that provide digital content and applications maintain ownership of their properties and can delete these at any time if they so choose. In* The Future of the Internet—and How to Stop It, *law professor Jonathan Zittrain holds that governments in the future may use such "tethered" technology to control information. Of course the existence of digitized media does not necessarily increase the likelihood of book banning: efforts at censorship long predate the electronic media age, and attempts to ban works on the basis of copyright infringement will continue. Nevertheless, electronic technology makes it theoretically possible to delete works consid-*

ered objectionable for one reason or another. To protect against such a future, consumers should demand that Amazon and other companies remove the means to alter or delete electronic content remotely.

Let's give [Internet retail giant] Amazon the benefit of the doubt—its explanation for why it deleted some books from customers' Kindles actually sounds halfway defensible. Last week [July 17, 2010] a few Kindle owners awoke to discover that the company had reached into their devices and remotely removed copies of George Orwell's *Nineteen Eighty-Four* and *Animal Farm*. Amazon explained that the books had been mistakenly published, and it gave customers a full refund. It turns out that Orwell wasn't the first author to get flushed down the Kindle's memory hole. In June, fans of Ayn Rand suffered the same fate—Amazon removed *Atlas Shrugged, The Fountainhead*, and *The Virtue of Selfishness*, with an explanation that it had "recently discovered a problem" with the titles. And some customers have complained of the same experience with *Harry Potter* books. Amazon says the Kindle versions of all these books were illegal. Someone uploaded bootlegged copies using the Kindle Store's self-publishing system, and Amazon was only trying to look after publishers' intellectual property. The Orwell incident was too rich with irony to escape criticism, however. Amazon was forced to promise that it will no longer delete its customers' books.

If Apple or Amazon can decide to delete stuff you've bought, then surely a court—or, to channel [George] Orwell, perhaps even a totalitarian regime—could force them to do the same.

Orwell Incident Has Profound Implications

Don't put too much stock in that promise. The worst thing about this story isn't Amazon's conduct; it's the company's technical capabilities. Now we know that Amazon can delete anything it wants from your electronic reader. That's an awesome power, and Amazon's justification in this instance is beside the point. As our media libraries get converted to 1's and 0's, we are at risk of losing what we take for granted today: full ownership of our book and music and movie collections.

Most of the e-books, videos, video games, and mobile apps that we buy these days aren't really ours. They come to us with digital strings that stretch back to a single decider—Amazon, Apple, Microsoft, or whomever else. [Apple CEO] Steve Jobs has confirmed that every iPhone routinely checks back with Apple to make sure the apps you've purchased are still kosher; Apple reserves the right to kill any app at any time for any reason. But why stop there? If Apple or Amazon can decide to delete stuff you've bought, then surely a court—or, to channel Orwell, perhaps even a totalitarian regime—could force them to do the same. Like a lot of others, I've predicted the Kindle is the future of publishing. Now we know what the future of book banning looks like, too.

Terms of Digital Ownership Are Different

Consider the legal difference between purchasing a physical book and buying one for your Kindle. When you walk into your local Barnes & Noble to pick up a paperback of *Animal Farm*, the store doesn't force you to sign a contract limiting your rights. If the Barnes & Noble later realizes that it accidentally sold you a bootlegged copy, it can't compel you to give up the book—after all, it's your property. The rules are completely different online. When you buy a Kindle a book, you're implicitly agreeing to Amazon's Kindle terms of service. The contract gives the company "the right to modify, suspend, or discontinue the Service at any time, and Amazon will not be liable to you should it exercise such right." In Amazon's view, the books you buy aren't your property—they're part of a "service," and Amazon maintains complete control of that service at all times. Amazon has similar terms covering downloadable movies and TV shows, as does Apple for stuff you buy from iTunes.

The difference between today's Kindle deletions and yesteryear's banning is that the earlier prohibitions weren't perfectly enforceable.

In *The Future of the Internet and How To Stop It*, Harvard law professor Jonathan Zittrain argues that such "tethered" appliances give the government unprecedented power to reach into our homes and change how our devices function. In 2004, TiVo sued Echostar (which runs Dish Network) for giving its customers DVR [digital video recorder] set-top boxes that TiVo alleged infringed on its software patents. A federal district judge agreed. As a remedy, the judge didn't simply force Dish to stop selling new devices containing the infringing software—the judge also ordered Dish to electronically disable the 192,000 devices that it had *already* installed in people's homes. (An appeals court later stayed the order; the legal battle is ongoing.) In 2001, a company called Playmedia sued AOL for including a version of the company's MP3 player in its software. A federal court agreed and ordered AOL to remove Playmedia's software from its customers' computers through a "live update."

The digitization of media doesn't necessarily make it more likely for books to get banned. Art is banned across the world for all kinds of reasons. In the United States, the usual justification is copyright infringement. Earlier this month, for instance, a judge issued an injunction against the publication of a Swedish author's unauthorized "sequel" to J.D. Salinger's *The Catcher in the Rye*. For other examples, take a look at *Stay Free!* magazine's collection of "illegal art": You'll find Todd Haynes' 1987 film *Superstar: The Karen Carpenter Story*, which played at several film festivals before all copies were ordered recalled and destroyed (Haynes hadn't obtained legal clearance for the music in the film); a CD's worth of songs shot down due to allegations of unlicensed sampling; and lots of parody comics—including of *Family Circus* and *Mickey Mouse*—that never saw the light of day.

The difference between today's Kindle deletions and yesteryear's banning is that the earlier prohibitions weren't perfectly enforceable. At best, publishers that found their books banned by courts could try to recall all books in circulation. In 2007, Cambridge University Press settled a lawsuit with Khalid bin Mahfouz, a Saudi Arabian banker who sued for libel over a book that alleged he'd funded terrorism. Cambridge agreed to ask libraries across the world to remove books from their shelves. But the libraries were free to refuse. If bin Mahfouz had sued over a Kindle book, on the other hand, he could ask the court not only to stop sales but also to delete all copies that had already been sold. As Zittrain points out, courts might consider such a request a logical way to enforce a ban—if they can order Dish Network to disable your DVR, they can also tell Amazon or Apple to disable a certain book, movie, or song.

The power to delete your books, movies, and music remotely is a power no one should have.

But that sets up a terrible precedent. Amazon deleted books that were already available in print, but in our paperless future—when all books exist as files on servers—courts would have the power to make works vanish completely. Zittrain writes: "Imagine a world in which all copies of once-censored books like *Candide* [by Voltaire], *The Call of the Wild* [by Jack London], and *Ulysses* [by James Joyce] had been permanently destroyed at the time of the censoring and could not be studied or enjoyed after subsequent decision-makers lifted the ban." This may sound like an exaggeration; after all, we'll surely always have file-sharing networks and other online repositories for works that have been decreed illegal. But it seems like small comfort to rely on BitTorrent to save banned art. The anonymous underground movements that have long sustained banned works will be a lot harder to keep up in the world of the Kindle and the iPhone.

Laws Lag Behind Technology

The power to delete your books, movies, and music remotely is a power no one should have. Here's one way around this: Don't buy a Kindle until Amazon updates its terms of service to prohibit remote deletions. Even better, the company ought to remove the technical capability to do so, making such a mass evisceration impossible in the event that a government compels it. (Sony and Interead—makers of rival e-book readers—didn't immediately respond to my inquiries about whether their devices allow the same functions. As far as I can tell, their terms of service don't give the companies the same blanket right to modify their services at will, though.)

But these problems are bigger than a few select companies. As Zittrain points out, they come about because of the law's inability to deal with tethered technology—devices that are both yours and not yours, in your possession but under the orders of companies far away. Amazon's promise to do better next time is going to be pretty hard to keep. The company says it won't delete any more books—but it hasn't said what it will do when someone alleges that one of its titles is libelous or violates someone else's copyright. This is bound to happen sooner or later, and the company might find itself deleting books once more. To solve this problem, what we really need are new laws.

Organizations to Contact

The editors have compiled the following list of organizations concerned with the issues debated in this book. The descriptions are derived from materials provided by the organizations. All have publications or information available for interested readers. The list was compiled on the date of publication of the present volume; names, addresses, phone and fax numbers, and e-mail and Internet addresses may change. Be aware that many organizations take several weeks or longer to respond to inquiries, so allow as much time as possible.

American Civil Liberties Union (ACLU)
125 Broad St., 18th Floor, New York, NY   10004
(212) 549-2500 • fax: (212) 549-2646
e-mail: aclu@aclu.org
website: www.aclu.org

The ACLU is a national organization that defends Americans' civil rights as guaranteed in the US Constitution. It advocates for freedom of all forms of speech, including pornography, flag burning, and political protest. The ACLU offers numerous reports, fact sheets, blog posts, and policy statements on free speech issues, which are freely available on its website. Some of these publications include "Free Speech Under Fire," "Freedom of Expression," and, for students, "Ask Sybil Liberty About Your Right to Free Expression."

American Library Association (ALA)
50 E. Huron Street, Chicago, IL   60611
(800) 545-2433 • fax: (312) 440-9374
e-mail: ala@ala.org
website: www.ala.org

The ALA is the primary professional organization for librarians in the United States. Through its Office for Intellectual Freedom (OIF), the ALA supports free access to libraries and library materials. The OIF also monitors and opposes efforts to ban books from libraries. Its publications, which are freely available on its website, include "Intellectual Freedom and Censorship Q & A," the "Library Bill of Rights," and the "Freedom to Read Statement."

Canadian Association for Free Expression (CAFE)

P.O. Box 332 Station 'B,' Etobicoke
Ontario   M9W 5L3
  Canada
(905) 897-7221 • fax: (905) 277-3914
e-mail: cafe@canadafirst.net
website: http://www.canadianfreespeech.com

CAFE, one of Canada's leading civil liberties groups, works to strengthen the freedom of speech and freedom of expression provisions in the Canadian Charter of Rights and Freedoms. It lobbies politicians and researches threats to freedom of speech. Publications include specialized reports, leaflets, and *The Free Speech Monitor*, a newsletter that is published ten times per year.

Eagle Forum

16 Pennsylvania Avenue SE, Suite 203
Washington, DC   20003
(202) 544-0353 • fax: (202) 547-6996
e-mail: eagle@eagleforum.org
website: www.eagleforum.org

Founded by Phyllis Schlafly in 1972, Eagle Forum is an organization that promotes the efforts of conservative and "pro-family" men and women to participate in the process of self-government and public policy making. Among other political objectives, Eagle Forum supports various tenets of what it calls "traditional education," including the rights of parents to guide the education of their own children and protect their children against instruction and materials they deem immoral. Eagle Forum's publications include *Education Reporter: The Newspaper of Education Rights*, which is freely available online and includes book reviews and regular coverage of book challenges and other news items that are archived under the heading "Bad Books."

Family Research Council (FRC)
801 G Street NW, Washington, DC   20001
(202) 393-2100 • fax: (202) 393-2134
website: www.frc.org

The Family Research Council is a faith-based organization that seeks to promote marriage and family. It believes that pornography harms women, children, and families, and therefore the FRC seeks to strengthen current obscenity laws. The organization maintains a blog at its website. It also publishes a variety of books, policy papers, fact sheets, and other materials, including the brochures "Dealing with Pornography: A Practical Guide for Protecting Your Family and Your Community" and "Internet Guide for Parents."

First Amendment Center at Vanderbilt University
1207 18th Ave. S., Nashville, TN   37212
(615) 727-1600 • fax: (615) 727-1319
e-mail: info@fac.org
website: http://www.firstamendmentcenter.org/

The First Amendment Center works to preserve and protect First Amendment freedoms through information and education. The center serves as a forum for the study and exploration of free-expression issues, including freedom of speech, the press, and religion, as well as the rights to assemble and to petition the government.

Foundation for Individual Rights in Education (FIRE)
601 Walnut St., Suite 510, Philadelphia, PA   19106
(215) 717-3473 • fax: (215) 717-3440
e-mail: fire@thefire.org
website: www.thefire.org

FIRE was founded in 1999 to defend the rights of students and professors at American colleges and universities. The group advocates for and provides legal assistance to students and professors who feel that their individual rights, particularly their rights to free speech, have been violated. The FIRE website features a blog titled "The Torch," as well as "Spotlight: The Campus Freedom Resource," a database containing information about speech codes at specific colleges and universities. The organization also publishes a quarterly newsletter and various guides to student rights, including *FIRE's Guide to Free Speech on Campus*.

Freedom Forum

1101 Wilson Blvd., Arlington, VA   22209
(703) 528-0800 • fax: (703) 284-3770
e-mail: news@freedomforum.org
website: www.freedomforum.org

The Freedom Forum was founded in 1991 to defend a free press and free speech. It operates the Newseum (a museum of news and the news media) and the First Amendment Center, which works to educate the public about free speech and other First Amendment issues. Its publications include an annual "State of the First Amendment" survey and various books, including *First Freedoms: A Documentary History of First Amendment Rights in the U.S.*, and *The First Amendment in Schools*. The First Amendment Center maintains on its website a "First Amendment Library" that serves as a clearinghouse for judicial, legislative, and other material on First Amendment freedoms.

Gateways to Better Education

P.O. Box 514, Lake Forest, CA   92609-0514
(949) 586-5437 • fax: (949) 457-6361
e-mail: info@gtbe.org
website: www.gtbe.org

Founded in 1991, Gateways is a non-profit organization that promotes a "faith-friendly" atmosphere in American public schools. Through seminars, lesson plans, and various other forms of advocacy, Gateways provides support to parents, teachers, and administrators for teaching Judeo-Christian history, ideas, and values in the classroom. Gateways' publications include the handbooks "Keeping the Faith in Public Schools" and "Expressing God's Love at School," as well as a bimonthly online newsletter.

Morality in Media (MIM)
475 Riverside Drive, Suite 1264, New York, NY   10115
(212) 870-3222 • fax: (212) 870-2765
e-mail: mim@moralityinmedia.org
website: http://www.moralityinmedia.org

MIM is a national interfaith organization that fights obscenity and indecency in the media. It works to educate the public on obscenity issues and maintains the National Obscenity Law Center, a clearinghouse of legal materials on obscenity law. Its publications include the reports "Stranger in the House: Reclaiming the Decency Today's Media Has Abandoned" and "Pornography's Effects on Adults and Children" and the quarterly *Morality in Media Newsletter*.

National Coalition Against Censorship (NCAC)
19 Fulton St. Suite 407, New York, NY   10038
(212) 807-6222 • fax: (212) 807-6245
e-mail: ncac@ncac.org
website: www.ncac.org

The NCAC is an alliance of national not-for-profit organizations, including literary, artistic, religious, educational, professional, labor, and civil liberties groups. The coalition works to defend freedom of thought, inquiry, and expression and to fight censorship. Its website provides access to press releases, legal briefs, and Congressional testimony on censorship issues.

Parents Against Bad Books in Schools (PABBIS)
4326 Ferry Landing Rd, Alexandria, VA   22309
(703) 360-8853 • fax: (703) 360-8853
e-mail: pabbis@pabbis.com
website: www.pabbis.org

PABBIS promotes the removal of controversial material from public schools and is located in Virginia. PABBIS believes that schools should not infringe on a family's religious beliefs and values. In an effort to sustain parents' right to protect children from offensive material, PABBIS supports parental activism concerning books that offend individual values within school systems. As a resource for parents, the organization publishes a "List of Lists" containing titles of more than 1,300 challenged or controversial books.

PEN American Center

588 Broadway, Suite 303, New York, NY   10012
(212) 334-1660 • fax: (212) 334-2181
e-mail: pen@pen.org
website: www.pen.org

PEN American Center is the US branch of International PEN, the world's oldest international literary and human rights organization. Among its many initiatives, PEN conducts a Freedom to Write Program, which engages in global advocacy efforts to defend writers who are imprisoned, endangered, or persecuted for their work and protect the freedom of the written word wherever it is threatened. The program mobilizes PEN Members and supporters to confront local, national, and regional threats to freedom of expression. PEN also champions international authors through *PEN America*, a semi-annual literary journal. The organization's other publications include a variety of reports and an electronic newsletter.

People for the American Way (PFAW)

2000 M Street, NW, Suite 400, Washington, DC   20036
(202) 467-4999 • fax: (202) 293-2672
e-mail: pfaw@pfaw.org
website: http://www.pfaw.org

PFAW works to promote citizen participation in democracy and safeguard the principles of the US Constitution, including the right to free speech. The organization maintains a blog and publishes a variety of fact sheets, articles, and position statements on its website.

Townhall.com

1901 N. Moore Street, Suite 701, Arlington, VA   22209
(703) 247-6046
e-mail: info@townhall.com

Townhall.com was launched in 1995 as the first conservative web community. Townhall split off from the Heritage Foundation in 2005, expanding the scope of its mission to inform, empower, and mobilize citizens for political change. Town hall.com pulls together news and political commentary from a vast array of partner organizations and columnists with the purpose of amplifying conservative voices in America's political debates.

Bibliography

Books

Robert Atkins and Svetlana Mintcheva, editors

Censoring Culture: Contemporary Threats to Free Expression. New York: The New Press, 2006.

Pamela Dell

You Can't Read This!: Why Books Get Banned. Mankato, MN: Compass Point Books, 2010.

Robert P. Doyle

Banned Books: Challenging Our Freedom to Read. Chicago: American Library Association, 2010.

Christopher M. Finan

From the Palmer Raids to the Patriot Act: A History of the Fight for Free Speech in America. Boston, MA: Beacon Press, 2007.

Marjorie Heins

Not in Front of the Children: "Indecency," Censorship, and the Innocence of Youth. Piscataway, NJ: Rutgers University Press, 2008.

Michelle M. Houle

Mark Twain: Banned, Challenged, and Censored. Berkeley Heights, NJ: Enslow Publishers, 2008.

Rebecca Knuth

Burning Books and Leveling Libraries: Extremist Violence and Cultural Destruction. Westport, CT: Praeger, 2006.

Anthony Lewis   *Freedom for the Thought That We Hate: A Biography of the First Amendment.* New York: Basic Books, 2007.

Joan Vos   *J.K. Rowling: Banned, Challenged, and Censored.* Berkeley Heights, NJ:
MacDonald   Enslow Publishers, 2008.

Sarah McNicol,   *Forbidden Fruit: The Censorship of Literature and Information for Young People.* Boca Raton, FL: Brown Walker Press, 2008
editor

Toni Morrison,   *Burn This Book: PEN Writers Speak out on the Power of the Word.* New York: HarperStudio, 2009
editor

Office for   *Intellectual Freedom Manual,* 8th
Intellectual   edition. Chicago: American Library
Freedom   Association, 2010.

R. Murray   *What Schools Ban and Why.*
Thomas   Westport, CT: Praeger, 2008.

Periodicals

Steve Baldwin   "Parents Protest American Library Association's 'Censorship,'" *Human Events,* January 17, 2006.

Phil Bildner   "Texas: If You Can't Ban Books, Ban Authors," *Time,* September 29, 2010.

Suzanne Bilyeu   "Mark Twain's Bad Boy," *The New York Times Upfront* 142 (March 1, 2010).

Fenice B. Boyd and Nancy M. Bailey — "Book Bans at Odds with Modernisation Efforts," *South China Morning Post*, February 8, 2008.

Fenice B. Boyd — "Censorship in Three Metaphors," *Journal of Adolescent & Adult Literacy* 52, no. 8 (May 2009): 653–61.

Brent Bozell — "Librarians against Censorship?" *Townhall*, May 9, 2008.

Kelsey Bradbury — "Authors of Teen Novels Defend Their Right to Tackle Tough Subjects," *Buffalo News*, September 27, 2006.

Neva Chonin — "The Bannish Inquisition," *San Francisco Chronicle*, October 1, 2006.

Deborah S. Connelly — "To Read or Not to Read: Understanding Book Censorship." *Community and Junior College Libraries* 15, no. 2 (2009): 83–90.

Kathy Edmondson — "Think for Yourself! Read Banned Books," *LaGrange Daily News*, October 25, 2010.

Beverly Goldberg — "Ban Violent Books from Prison Libraries, Urges Connecticut State Senator," *American Libraries* (online), October 12, 2010.

Erin Downey Howerton — "Just Open the Door: Banned Books (and a Librarian!) in the Classroom," *Young Adult Library Services*, spring 2007.

Leonard Kniffel   "Banning and Burning," *American Libraries*, October 1, 2010.

Sarah Darer Littman   "Book Banners Can Be Very Selective in Their Outrage," *The Advocate*, October 1, 2010.

Benedicte Page   "New *Huckleberry Finn* Edition Censors 'N-Word'," *Guardian*, January 5, 2011.

Molly Rosbach   "Banning Books Silences Learning Opportunities," *Mid-Columbia Voices*, September 29, 2010.

Scott Shane   "Pentagon Plan: Buying Books to Keep Secrets." *New York Times*, September 9, 2010.

Boyd Tonkin   "Censorship: Still a Burning Issue," *Independent*, February 22, 2007.

Index

3M